MURDER AS A BUSINESS DECISION

An Economic Analysis
of a Criminal Phenomena

Gary E. Marché

MURDER AS A BUSINESS DECISION

An Economic Analysis of a Criminal Phenomena

Gary E. Marché

Austin & Winfield, Publishers
San Francisco - London - Bethesda
1998

Library of Congress Cataloging-in-Publication Data

Marché, Gary E., 1953-
    Murder as a business decision : an economic analysis of a criminal
phenomena / Gary E. Marché.
    p. cm.
    Includes bibliographical references and index.
    ISBN 1-57292-120-X (alk. paper)
    1. Murder--United States. 2. Murder--United States--Psychological
aspects. I. Title.
HV6529.M36   1998
364.15'2--dc21   98-17072
                                                                 CIP

Editorial Inquiries:
Austin & Winfield, Publishers
7831 Woodmont Avenue, #345
Bethesda, MD 20814
(301) 654-7335

To Order: (800) 99-AUSTIN

To Mary and Élan

Contents

List of Illustrations

Figures

Tables

Preface

This book is about homicides that are committed for the purpose of gaining or maintaining wealth. Such homicides tend to be more carefully planned and they may derive greater efficiency from organizational specialization and greater certainty from enforced secrecy. Planned homicides suggest that the primary motivation to murder is based upon rational calculation. Economic models or theories avoid consideration of emotional behavior and do not necessarily assume moral behavior. Accordingly, economic models are clearly an advantage in this area of analysis. Moreover, economic analysis occupies the middle ground between the broader social context theories of sociology and the narrower motive related focus of psychology. As such, economic theory should play a dominant role in the analysis of all crimes that appear to be rationally motivated.

The primary motivation for writing this book is that homicide clearance rates have fallen from over 90% in 1960 to about 65 % today. Assuming that police investigative resources are sufficient and not wasted, this suggests technical inefficiency that can be viewed as a "hole in the police dragnet." The rationality element of murder as a business decision suggests that this type of homicide offender will continue to learn how to exploit opportunities for gain. In other words, highly experienced homicide offenders will continue to routinely pass through an ever widening "hole in the police dragnet." The downward trend in homicide clearance rates should be expected to continue unless there is an increase in technical efficiency by homicide investigators and in the production of convictions and punishment by other units of the criminal justice system.

The analysis in the textbook relies on economic theory and empirical analysis to generate specific suggestions for improving technical efficiency and increase the level of criminal justice system production in this area. It is hoped that the result will be to fix the "hole in the police dragnet" and, thereby, arrest the downward trend in homicide clearance rates originating in business based crimes.

INTRODUCTION

This book is about homicides that are committed for the purpose of enhancing profits or wealth. Net wealth gains cannot be achieved if the offender is apprehended, convicted and punished. Accordingly, such homicides tend to be more carefully considered and planned. Since consideration and planning exemplify rational calculation it is logical to infer that the primary basis for choosing the murder alternative is extensive rational calculation. The wealth objective tends to exclude other planned homicides such as those committed by serial-murderers or political terrorists whose objectives are generally different. Economic models or theories avoid consideration of emotional behavior and do not necessarily assume moral behavior. Therefore, economic models are clearly an advantage in this area of analysis. Moreover, economic analysis occupies the middle ground between the broader social context theories of sociology and the narrower motive related focus of psychology. As such, economic theory should play a dominant role in the analysis of all homicides in which the murder alternative is chosen on the basis of extensive rational calculation.

The primary motivation for writing this book is that homicide clearance rates have fallen from over 90% in 1960 to about 60% to 65% today. Some of the explanatory factors for this falling trend appear to include 1) increases in the proportion of offenders who are not related to their victims, 2) increases in the proportion of offenders who tend to be motivated by wealth gains and who choose the homicide alternative more on the basis of rational calculation, 3) organizational efficiencies gained by groups of wealth seeking offenders, 4) increases in gang activity, and 5) technical inefficiency in investigative processes.

The rationality element suggests that homicide offenders will continue to learn about opportunities and how to exploit them. In other words, highly experienced homicide offenders will continue to routinely pass through a "hole in the police dragnet." Consequently, the downward trend in homicide clearance rates should be expected to continue unless there is an increase in production by units of the criminal justice system. The economic analysis in the textbook generates specific suggestions for increasing the level of criminal justice system production in this area. Specific emphasis is placed on methods for improving allocative, cost, and technical efficiency in the production of apprehension, conviction and deterrence. It is hoped that the result will be to fix the "hole in the police dragnet" and, thereby, arrest the downward trend in homicide clearance rates.

The book is divided into two parts. Part I is an introduction to economics and criminal behavior in which the economic theory of choice is developed. Choice theory is then used to analyze and explain illegal speeding. Some resource allocation issues are also discussed. Part II builds on the material developed in Part I and develops the theory of murder as a business decision. Though the book is based on economic theory, empirical evidence and real examples are also provided.

Issues such as falling homicide clearance rates and planned homicides are those that primarily concern criminal justice students. On the other hand, the economic analysis of these subjects makes this truly an interdisciplinary textbook. Accordingly, the textbook is aimed at upper undergraduate and graduate level social scientists. Students should have taken at least principles of microeconomics and be familiar with basic calculus, introductory statistics, and research methodologies.

PART I.   AN INTRODUCTION TO ECONOMICS
           AND CRIMINAL BEHAVIOR

CHAPTER 1
CONSUMER CHOICE THEORY

This chapter develops the utility-maximizing consumer model or theory. The consumer model is a model of individual choice and is applicable to many different situations and types of choices. Its general applicability means that the consumer model can even provide the basis for the analysis of rationally motivated business-like murder. The analysis of murder as a business decision is developed in detail in later chapters. First, however, it is important to understand the nature of the consumer model or theory and it's assumptions. The purpose of Chapter 1 is to make the model (or theory) of the utility-maximizing consumer clear.

THE UTILITY MAXIMIZING CONSUMER

Economics is defined to be the study of how individuals make decisions about the allocation of their scarce resources in order to get the most out of them. Individual citizens can be aggregated to be an "individual" society. When "individual" refers to a society as a whole, macroeconomic analysis is sometimes applied. On the other hand, when decision makers are individual citizens and "individual" refers to just one person, microeconomic analysis is applicable.

Consumer choice theory is a major application of microeconomic theory involving individual choice. In order to be consistent with the definition of economics, consumer choice theory must be an analysis of scarce resource allocation. For consumers, scarce resources include incomes or budgets. It is hypothesized that an individual consumer's resources will be allocated (through decision choices) such that the greatest level of satisfaction or utility results.

In general, economic theories or models make widely applicable behavioral assertions. This applies to the consumer model as well. Typically it is asserted that individuals act rationally in the pursuit of some assumed objective or motive (such as utility maximization in the case of the consumer). Rational behavior means that the decision or choice maker (for example a consumer) is aware of and considers the expected consequences of alternative choices. Consequences are subdivided into benefits and costs and are evaluated within the context of an assumed objective such as utility maximization. Rational behavior appears logically necessary if it is assumed that some action, such as consumption, is necessary in order to gain greater satisfaction or utility. Consumption choices involve costs that may constrain or reduce net gains in utility. Thus only those consumption choices that are expected to have benefits greater than costs are considered to be rational. In other words, all rational choices must lead to a net increase in the consumer's utility or, equivalently, toward the achievement of the assumed objective.

Another way to look at consumer choice theory is to consider it in reverse order starting with the assumed objective of maximizing utility. If the consumer is always trying to make him or herself better off (that is, to increase net utility), then the consumer must become aware of opportunities to do so. Rational calculation that involves a comparison of the costs and benefits of the possible choices is required in order for the consumer to become aware of those particular opportunities that will make them better-off. Thus if the price (cost) of a wanted consumption item is lowered, a rational (and informed) consumer may determine that there is an opportunity to increase his or her utility. Observe, for example, how consumers behave when a good (not a "bad" such as dirt or mud) is given away for free.

An individual's tastes and preferences for a particular good or services determine the net effect that consumption has on utility. Good X, for example, may increase utility more for one consumer than for another. Good X may even be a "bad" for some individuals and decrease their utility. Do you consider heroin, for example, to be a "good" or a "bad"? It is assumed that interpersonal comparisons of utility cannot be made. An individual's tastes and preferences are assumed to have been formed over a long period of time and are unique to that individual. Only recently have economists actually tried to analyze specific factors that may account for taste. On the other hand, it has been established that consumers (at least those who are generally considered to be adults) tend to have tastes and preferences that are relatively consistent and predictable.

Given some specific and realistic assumptions about how the unobservable behavioral assertions relate to real objects, economic theories or models also predict that certain observable events will occur. For example, if it is assumed that all else is held constant (the ceteris paribus assumption), then a relative decrease in the price (marginal cost) of bread will be observed to increase the quantity of bread consumed. This is because the "rational zone" of consumption now includes an additional amount of marginal benefits (or utility) that exceed the now lower marginal cost (price) of consuming bread. Therefore, it is rational for individuals in the bread market to consume more bread. In other words, individuals who consider bread to be a good will determine, through rational calculation, that opportunities exist to improve their well-being. For a given individual, the consumption of bread is not predicted to continue into the "irrational zone" in which the price or marginal cost is perceived to become greater than the ever diminishing marginal benefits of successive loaves of bread consumed. In other words, rational consumers are not expected to voluntarily make choices in which they trade away money (marginal costs) for loafs of bread indefinitely.

To be useful as an economic model or theory the predicted events must be tested against real world data and it must be possible for the predicted events not to occur. In other words, an economic model or theory that cannot be refuted is not useful. Assuming that an economic model is not refuted empirically, it is also important to note that behavior that is consistent with an economic model can not prove that the unobservable behavior assertion of rationality is true. Since thinking or reasoning processes are not directly observable, individuals who make choices that are consistent with the predictions of an economic theory or model can only be said to be behaving as if they are rational.[1]

Total and Marginal Utility

Economic models of consumer behavior are good at predicting and explaining consumer behavior because they are based upon the generally applicable behavior assumptions of rationality, consistent preferences, and the broadly applicable objective of utility maximization. The objective (utility) function is broadly applicable because utility simply means the benefit or satisfaction gained by an individual from any specific action choice. In economics, examples of action choices typically involve consumption or production, but criminal action choices can also produce utility.

In reality, utility is subjectively evaluated and unique to each individual. However, in very abstract economic models[2] that are often intended to serve mostly pedagogical purposes, utility can be thought of as a measurable quantity. Measurable utility is also known as cardinal utility and acts as an additional simplifying assumption. The following example illustrates measurable or cardinal utility and involves the consumption of hamburgers and roller-coaster rides. First, assume that a consumer can wear a util meter that registers the utility gained in consumption in "utils." Suppose, for example, that the consumption of a hamburger generates a measurable 10 utils of satisfaction and the consumption of a roller coaster ride also generates 10 utils of satisfaction to the consumer. The consumer also finds that repeated consumption of the same good or service in a given period of time begins to yields smaller and smaller amounts of utility. In other words, the second unit consumed of roller-coaster rides or hamburgers are found to yield less than 10 utils of satisfaction. This is called diminishing marginal utility. Diminishing marginal utility means that total utility increases by diminishing amounts as successive units of the exact same good or service is consumed. The term "marginal" simply means the next incremental unit. Diminishing marginal utility can happen quickly for some goods and explains why you usually do not find more than one red pickup truck, for example, owned by the same individual.

Second, the consumer must have some scarce resources that can be used to obtain gains in utility. In this example the scarce resource is a consumer budget of $4.00.[3] Let the $4.00 consumer budget be represented by B = 4. To keep the example simple assume that there are only two goods or choices available: Hamburgers (H) and roller-coaster rides (R). The objective in this example is to derive or identify a consumer demand curve. In other words, we want to predict how the consumer will behave or relate to the real objects H and R under specific conditions. To derive a demand curve we will need the initial prices for hamburgers (H) and roller coaster rides (R), a second price for one of the two goods (that is, for either H or R), and the assumption that all other factors are held constant. Let the price of a hamburger (H) equal $1.00 and be designated as Ph = 1. The price of hamburgers will remain Ph = 1 throughout this example. Let the initial price of a roller-coaster ride (R) equal $2.00 and be designated as Pr = 2. Later, the price of roller coaster rides will fall to Pr = 1.

Table 1.1 illustrates the total, marginal, and per-dollar marginal utilities for the consumer. Table 1.1 also includes a column of per-dollar marginal utilities for the case in which the price of a roller-coaster ride (R) falls to $1.00 (Pr = 1).

10

Table 1.1

Measurable or Cardinal Utility (Utils)

Roller Coaster Rides: Hamburgers:

Total Utility (Utils)	Marg. Utility (MU = ΔTU/1)	Marg. Utility/ $ (Pr=2)	Marg. Utility/ $ (Pr=1)	Total Utility (Utils)	Marg. Utility (MU = ΔTU/1)	Marg. Utility/ $ (Ph=1)
1 Ride = 10 utils	10 utils	10 utils/$2 = 5 utils/$	10 utils/$1	1 Hamb. = 10 utils	10 utils	10 utils/$1
2 Rides = 15 utils	5 utils	5 utils/$2 = 2.5 utils/$	5 utils/$1	2 Hamb. = 15 utils	5 utils	5 utils/$1
3 Rides = 18 utils	3 utils	3 utils/$2 = 1.5 utils/$	3 utils/$1	3 Hamb. = 17 utils	2 utils	2 utils/$1
4 Rides = 20 utils	2 utils	2 utils/$2 = 1 utils/$	2 utils/$1	4 Hamb. = 17 utils	0 utils	0 utils/$1

Perfect information is an additional simplifying assumption and the consumer in this example is assumed to have it. Perfect information means that the consumer knows all prices (costs), measurable utilities (benefits), and all possible alternatives available. In other words, the consumer is highly informed. In decision making terminology, the consumer is completely certain of the consequences of each and every budget allocation choice. Thus the consumer will be able to choose optimally. That is he or she will be able to achieve the maximum utility possible from the scarce resources available.

Perfect information does not cause the model of consumer behavior to become unreasonably abstract if, in the real world, consumers tend to become more informed, as opposed to less informed, about the goods and services that they consume.

Note that saving is not an available choice in this example. It is not possible to choose the bundle 0R,0H and then use the entire budget, or any part of it, for savings. Instead the entire budget of B = 4 must be spent on the only utility producing goods available (H and R). Moreover, the assumed goal of maximizing utility means that the consumer's entire budget will continue to be used for the consumption of H and R as long as they remain "goods" (that is, generate positive marginal utility in consumption).

Starting with the initial prices of roller coaster rides of Pr = 2 and hamburgers Ph = 1 and the measured utility from table 1.1, all possible choices that the consumer can make with $4.00 can be illustrated as follows.

Choice	Quantity	Total Cost	Total Utility
C1:	2R,0H	$4.00	15+0 = 15 utils
C2:	1R,2H	$4.00	10+15 = 25 utils
C3:	0R,4H	$4.00	0+17 = 17 utils

Clearly, the maximum utility that can be gained from scarce resources B = 4 is 25 utils in choice C2. Since the consumer has perfect information and is assumed rational choice C2 is the one predicted to be made. Choice C2 is necessarily an optimal choice. Without perfect information or, equivalently, certainty in decision making, some of the available alternatives may not be known. Also, the consumer may not have a complete knowledge of prices (costs) or the exact number of utils (benefits) to be gained from a good or service. Without perfect information (i.e., thorough and complete information processing) the consumer will be more likely to make a suboptimal choice and achieve less satisfaction from his or her scarce resources.

With the prices of roller coaster rides at Pr = 2, hamburgers at Ph = 1 and all budget resources fully exhausted table 1.1 indicates that per-dollar marginal utility or "bang-for-the-buck" at the optimal choice (C2: 1R,2H) is equal for both goods at 5 utils/$. Although delineating the consequences of possible choices indicates that the optimal choice is C2, an analysis of per-dollar marginal utility is another way to illustrate the optimal resource allocation problem for the consumer. For example, choice C1: 2R,0H is not an optimal choice because it reflects an over-allocation of budget resources to roller-coaster rides (R) and an under-allocation of resources towards hamburgers (H). More specifically, per-dollar marginal utility obtained for R at C1: 2R,0H is only 2.5 utils/$. If the consumer had chosen differently and allocated his or her budget resources towards the consumption of more hamburgers (H) and fewer roller coaster rides (R), per-dollar marginal utility would be 10 utils/$ for the first hamburger (H). Thus, by simply re-allocating scarce dollars away from the over consumed and low "bang-for-the-buck" item (R) and toward the underconsumed and high "bang-for-the-buck" item (H) the consumer would be able to derive greater utility or "bang" per dollar. In terms of the available choices, such a reallocation would increase the consumer's total utility from 15 utils for choice C1: 2R,0H to 25 utils for choice C2: 1R,2H.

Choice C3: 0R,4H is the other choice extreme in which one of the two goods is not consumed at all. Choice C3: 0R,4H exhausts all budget resources but it indicates low "bang-for-the-buck" or an overallocation of resources towards hamburgers (H) and high "bang-for-the-buck" if resources were re-allocated toward greater consumption of roller-coaster rides (R). Re-allocating resources so that per dollar marginal utilities or "bang-for-the-buck" are equal would increase total utility from 17 utils for C3: 0R,4H to 25 utils for choice C2: 1R,2H.

The utility maximization rule is always to allocate each dollar so as to get the greatest marginal utility or "band-for-the-buck" from it in consumption. Diminishing marginal utility then assures that the consumer will then end up maximizing the utility from his or her scarce resources or budget.. As a mathematical condition, total utility is maximized when there is equal marginal utility per dollar for each good consumed at the point at which all income is completely exhausted. That is, when $MU_1/P_1 = MU_2/P_2 = \ldots = MU_n/P_n$ for all goods and services 1 through n.

In the real world the consumer's assessment of the difference in value between the utility maximization condition and suboptimal choices provides a material incentive for consumers to acquire information. Direct investment in the stock market provides a good example of the value of information. Notice how most stock market investors are always trying to acquire better information. How much more could you make in stocks if you new the consequences of each choice with certainty?

The all else held constant (or ceteris paribus) assumption means that all other factors that might influence the way the consumer relates to a given real object are assumed to be held constant. These factors are the consumers' resources or budget (B = 4), the prices of other goods, and the consumer's tastes and preferences. Let the price of a roller-coaster ride now be set at $1.00 so that Pr = 1. Just as when Pr = 2, the model of consumer behavior will predict how the consumer will relate to the real object roller-coaster rides (R) under the specific conditions that all other factors that might influence consumer behavior have been held constant. In this case the price of the other good (H) will remain constant at Ph = 1, the budget will remain at B = 4, and the consumer's tastes (generally assumed stable) will be very unlikely to have changed in this relatively short period of time.

When the price of roller coaster rides is Pr = 1 the consumer is expected to make the optimal consumption choice. As before, all budget resources will continue to be used for consumption as long as saving is not an available choice and the two goods (H) and (R) yield positive marginal utility. There are now five possible choices or bundles of hamburgers (H) and roller coaster rides (R) at Pr = Ph = 1. These can be delineated as follows:

Choice	Quantity	Total Cost	Total Utility
C1:	4R,0H	$4.00	20+0 = 20 utils
C2:	3R,1H	$4.00	18+10 = 28 utils
C3:	2R,2H	$4.00	15+15 = 30 utils
C4:	1R,3H	$4.00	10+17 = 27 utils
C5:	0R,4H	$4.00	0+17 = 17 utils

The choice that now gains the consumer the greatest level of utility or satisfaction is choice C3: 2R,2H. For the optimal choice C3: 2R,2H per-dollar marginal utility for both goods is equal at 5 utils/$ when all budget resources are completely exhausted.

The way that the consumer has related to the real object roller coaster rides (R) under specific conditions is described by the demand curve for good (R). The demand curve for roller coaster rides (R) can now be derived because we have two prices for R, Pr = 2 and Pr = 1, and two quantities, Qr = 1 and Qr = 2. The two quantities are obtained from the two optimal choice bundles. That is when Pr = 2 the optimal choice was C2: 1R,2H and when Pr = 1 the optimal choice was C3: 2R,2H. Thus the decrease in the price of roller coaster ride price from Pr = 2 to Pr = 1, all else held constant, resulted in an increase in the quantity of roller coaster rides consumed from 1R to 2R. Demand curves are assumed to have a negative or downward slope and indicate an inverse relationship between prices and quantities. The demand curve for roller coaster rides (R) is labeled D_1 in figure 1.1. With perfect information, the price/quantity pairs along D_1 reflect optimal consumer choices, all else held constant.

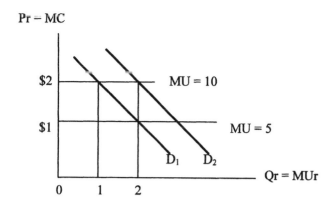

Pr = MC

$2 — — — — MU = 10

$1 — — — — MU = 5

D₁   D₂

0   1   2   Qr = MUr

Fig. 1.1. Consumer Demand for Roller-Coaster Rides. When Pr falls from $2 to $1 on D_1 the consumer increases consumption from 1 ride to 2 rides, all other factors held constant. The downward sloping demand curve D_1 reflects assumed diminishing marginal utility (benefits) in that MU = 10 at Q = 1 to MU = 5 at Q = 2. Notice that MU = 10 at Q = 2 on the higher level of demand curve D_2. On either demand curve, opportunities in consumption occur only when D ≥ Pr or, equivalently, when MU ≥ MC.

Along the downward sloping demand curve D_1 the marginal utility or benefits of successive amounts consumed are assumed to be diminishing. Referring to the marginal utility column in table 1.1, marginal utility for one roller-coaster ride is 10 utils and marginal utility for two roller-coaster rides is 5 utils. Thus a downward sloping demand curve is also a diminishing marginal utility or benefit curve and reflects the incentive or opportunity that a consumer has to gain net benefits through the act of consumption. Note that demand curve D_1 implies that consumption will continue to occur as long as the demand curve or, equivalently, the level of marginal utility or benefit is greater than or equal to price Pr.

When demand curves shift to the right, such as D_1 to D_2, there is said to be an increasing change in demand for roller-coaster rides (R). A change or shift in demand can only be caused by a change in one or more of the factors otherwise held constant. Thus a change in hamburger prices (Ph), the consumer's budget (B), or the consumers' tastes and preferences could cause the demand curve to shift or change to a new position. On the other hand, a change in the price of roller coaster rides (Pr) cannot cause the demand curve for roller coaster rides to shift. A change in the price of Pr automatically invokes the all else held constant assumption and can, therefore, only cause a change in the quantity demand along a given demand curve.

For any given quantity of roller coaster rides (R) consumed, it is important to note that the level of marginal utility on demand curve D_2 is greater than the corresponding level of marginal utility on demand curve D_1. Thus an increase in the consumer's budget that resulted in an increase in the level of demand for roller coaster rides from D_1 to D_2 would indicate that the consumer could gain an increase in total utility at any given price. In other words, the consumer model predicts that you can have more fun with more money!

As indicated, demand curve D_1 indicates an inverse relationship between the quantity of roller coaster rides consumed (Qr) and the price of roller coaster rides (Pr). However, an inverse relationship between Pr and Qr might not be so clearly observed if all else is not held constant--that is, if the consumer relates to real object R under non-specific circumstances. For example, a decrease in the consumer's budget and a corresponding leftward shift in the demand curve that occurred at the same time as a decrease in price might make the inverse relationship between price and quantity demanded difficult to observe. The decrease in the budget would tend to reduce consumption at all price levels and the decrease in price would to increase quantity demanded. If the two effects were exactly offsetting, one might conclude that a decrease in price does not lead to an increase in the quantity consumed. This makes the all else held constant assumption very important. Often the only way to correctly observe a demand curve in the real world is through a combination of real world data and appropriate statistical techniques. Appropriate statistical, or empirical, techniques will provide the means to invoke the assumption of all else held constant.

Figure 1.1 can be used to illustrate the important concept of rational choice. As indicated, rational behavior implies that only those choices with benefits (utility) greater than costs will be considered. By definition, the benefits or "good" consequences of a choice move the consumer closer to his or her assumed goal of utility maximization. Costs, on the other hand, act as constraints to achieving this goal. In figure 1.1, an infinitely divisible set of utility producing choices is depicted as the smoothly drawn, downward sloping consumer demand curve. The demand curve has a downward or negative slope because diminishing marginal benefits (utilities) are assumed. With price (Pr) equal to the marginal cost of each choice, only those choices with marginal benefits greater than Pr would be considered to be rational choices. Along a given demand curve, lowering Pr from 2 to 1 simply makes a greater set of consumption choices rational to choose. Since the set of rational choices for hamburgers has remained constant (that is, Ph, B, and the consumer's preferences are assumed constant), this is predicted to lead to the greater consumption of roller-coaster rides (R).

Note that a perfectly informed consumer does not engage in the act of consumption in the irrational zone on any demand curve. Along demand curve D_1 the irrational zone is when $Pr > D_1$. When $Pr > D_1$, the consumer would consider the marginal costs of consumption to be greater than the marginal benefits (that is, MC > MU). Consequently, consumption in the "irrational zone" would make the consumer worse-off because only net losses in utility would occur.

The way the consumption of roller-coaster rides (R) is related to the consumer's gains in total utility (TU) is summarized by the utility function (U) in figure 1.2. When marginal consumption choices are limited to roller-coaster rides R only, the utility function can be written simply as $U = U(R)$. This means that total utility (TU) or (U) is determined by the consumption of roller coaster rides (R) only. The upward sloping utility function (U) in figure 1.2 indicates that increases in roller coaster rides (R) increase total utility or benefits. The upward slope of (U) simply defines (R) to be a "good," as opposed to a "bad," over this range of the consumer's utility function. Cost considerations are not defined by utility functions and are not depicted in figure 1.2.

18

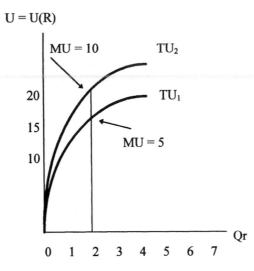

$U = U(R)$

MU = 10   TU₂

20   TU₁

15

MU = 5

10

0 1 2 3 4 5 6 7   Qr

Fig.1.2. Roller-Coaster Ride Utility Function (Measurable Utility). The utility functions $U = U(R)$ that correspond to D_1 and D_2 in figure 1.1 are depicted by the two curves TU_1 and TU_2. $U = U(R)$ reflects increasing total utility (TU) as units of R are consumed in a given period of time. Diminishing marginal utilities in consumption are reflected by the diminishing slopes of TU_1 and TU_2. At any number of units of R consumed the slope of the utility function TU_1 (at that exact point) is the same value as the level of marginal utility in demand curve D_1 in figure 1.1. The same is true for TU_2 and D_2. The utility function TU_2 has a greater slope and marginal utility value at any quantity consumed (Qr) than does utility function TU_1.

Figure 1.2 illustrates the utility function $U = U(R)$ in terms of the "util" values in table 1.1 and the two demand curves D_1 and D_2 in figure 1.1. In table 1.1, the level of total utility is given by the number of utils of total utility gained from the number of units of roller coaster rides (R) consumed. In figure 1.2, total utility (TU or U) is the height of the utility function at the total number of units of roller coaster rides (R) consumed. At a given number of roller coaster rides (R) consumed the slope of the utility function (U) is equal to the value of marginal utility (MU). The assumption of diminishing marginal utility causes the slope of the utility function to be positive yet decreasing. In mathematical terms diminishing marginal utility means that, at any point, the first derivative of the utility function (U) is positive (that is, U' > 0) and, at the same point, the change in the slope of (U) as determined by the second derivative of (U) is negative (that is, U" < 0).

In figure 1.2 the utility function TU_1 corresponds to demand curve D_1 in figure 1.1 and utility function TU_2 corresponds to demand curve D_2. Note that the slope and, hence, marginal utility at any quantity of roller coaster rides (R) consumed is greater on TU_2 than on TU_1. Assuming that increased budget resources (B) caused an increase in demand for roller coaster rides (R) from D_1 and D_2 in figure 1.1, figure 1.2 and the two utility curves TU_1 and TU_2 indicate that increased budget resources (B) allow the consumer to gain greater total utility or benefits.

Utility Ranking

Unlike the previous example the level of satisfaction or utility gained from an action such as consumption is not really measurable. Instead, utility is a subjectively determined value and depends on an individual's preferences for particular goods and services. Because utility cannot be measured and because preferences or tastes are observed to vary between individuals, the utility gained from the consumption of a particular good is not subject to interpersonal comparison. If, however, the consumer is able to rank the different possible bundles of R and H (that is, different choices) according to his or her own particular preferences, then the same demand curve can be obtained as in figure 1.1. In other words, the consumer will still relate to the real object roller coaster rides (R) in response to a change in the price of roller coaster rides (Pr)in the same way as before, all else held constant.

Suppose, for example, that the consumer is able to say that the consumption bundle 2R,2H yields a higher level of utility or satisfaction than consumption bundle 1R,2H. In this case then the consumer prefers the bundle or choice 2R,2H more than 1R,2H. This particular preference ranking makes sense if it is assumed that roller coaster rides (R) continue to yield positive marginal utility. The consumer may also be able to identify different consumption bundles (choice alternatives) that yield the same level of utility or satisfaction as either of the two bundles 1R,2H and 2R,2H. In other words, there are some other bundles or combinations of R and H that the consumer prefers equally to bundle 1R,2H and there are also some other bundles of R and H that the consumer prefers equally to bundle 2R,2H.

Bundles that yield the same level of utility lie along an "indifference" curve that is convex to the origin. Along the indifference curve, the consumer is assumed to be willing to trade away one good in exchange for an exactly compensating amount of the other good. Thus the consumer is always willing to consume more of a given good along an indifference curve. The required trade-off between goods means that indifference curves have a negative slope. Indifference curves are convex to the origin and have no flat spots if they reflect decreasing marginal values for any good as more of that good is consumed. In other words, the consumer's willingness to voluntarily trade or substitute one good for the other good is decreasing even though "more is preferred to less" for any good.

Decreasing marginal rates of (voluntary) substitution provides the possibility of illustrating the "constrained-income utility-maximization" problem in which there is a unique optimal solution for each of the two roller-coaster ride prices (Pr =2 and Pr = 1) as in figure 1.3. It is assumed that the consumer has consistent preferences and, consequently, that indifference curves do not cross. Consistent preferences mean that the indifference curves will always retain the capability of ranking the level of utility of one set of equally preferred bundles against another set of equally preferred bundles that yield a different level of utility.

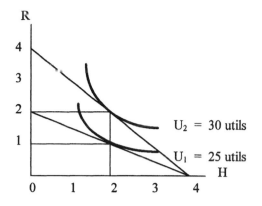

Fig. 1.3. Constrained Utility-Maximization for two goods (R) and (H). The indifference curves (U) represent indexes of total utility or satisfaction such that any consumption bundle R,H on U_2 is defined to be a higher level of total utility than any consumption bundle R,H on U_1. The measurable or cardinal utility (utils) used in table 1.1 can be assumed to correspond to the ordinal utility indexes as indicated. That is, the higher index of satisfaction U_2 corresponds to 30 utils and the lower index of satisfaction U_1 corresponds to 25 utils. Given the budget constraints associated with either Pr = 2 and Pr = 1, the optimal choice is indicated by the points of tangency (A and B) between the relevant budget constraint and the highest possible indifference curve attainable.

Even though the budget or level of income is always held constant, figure 1.3 has two budget constraints. This is because the price of roller coaster rides varies and the two budget constraints reflect the possible quantities or bundles of R and H that can be attained at each of the two prices. Thus when B = 4, Ph = 1, and Pr = 2 the three possible choice bundles (2R,0H), (1R,2H), and (0R,4H) all lie along the lower budget constraint line. When B = 4, Ph=1 and the price of roller coaster rides falls to Pr = 1, the budget constraint line rotates up and to the right to reflect five possible choice bundles: (4R,0H), (3R,1H), (2R,2H), (1R,3H) and (0R,4H). Note that all choices on each budget line completely exhaust all available budget resources. Given B, Ph, and Pr, choice bundles that lie outside the budget "constraint" line are clearly not possible. Also, saving is not defined to be a good. Therefore, any choice bundles that lie inside a given budget line must leave as unused or wasted some budget resources that could otherwise be used by the consumer to gain additional utility (benefits).

A method for calculating the set of possible alternatives that exhaust all budget resources is to use a budget or expenditure equation such as

$$B = Pr(R) + Ph(H). \tag{1.1}$$

Given values for B, Pr, and Ph, expenditure equation (1.1) indicates the number of units of R and H that can be consumed. For example, if B = 4, Pr = 2, and Ph = 1, the expenditure equation (1.1) requires that if R equals 1 then H must equal 2.

$$4 = 2(R) + 1(H)$$
$$4 = 2(1) + 1(H)$$
$$H = 2 \, .$$

Similarly, if R equals 2 then H must equal zero and if R equal zero then H must equal 4.

$$4 = 2(2) + 1(H) \qquad\qquad 4 = 2(0) + 1(H)$$
$$H = 0 \qquad\qquad\qquad\qquad H = 4$$

This gives us the three possible choices of R and H associated Pr = 2. By changing Pr from 2 to 1, all else held constant, the second set of five possible choices for R and H can be determined.

Alternatively, by rearranging equation (1.1) the budget constraint lines can be written in a linear equation, slope-intercept form as

$$R = (B/Pr) - (Ph/Pr)H \tag{1.2}$$

where (B/Pr) is the R axis intercept and -(Ph/Pr) is the slope. For example, plugging in the values of B = 4, Pr = 2, and Pr = 1 into the slope-intercept equation (1.2) gives

$$R = (4/2) - (1/2)H = 2 - (1/2)H$$

which means that the intercept on the R axis is at 2 units (that is, two roller coaster rides) and the slope of the budget constraint line is - (1/2). The negative slope of - (1/2) means that one roller coaster ride can be purchased by trading away two hamburgers. All possible consumer choices of R and H that completely exhaust the consumer's budget must lie along this line.

Similarly, when Pr = 1 equation (1.2) gives the new budget line

$$R = (4/1) - (1/1)H = 4 - 1H.$$

Decreasing the price of R from Pr = 2 to Pr = 1 causes the budget line to rotate clock-wise so that the R intercept increases from 2 to 4 and the negative slope becomes steeper. The steeper, negative slope requires that now only one hamburger needs to be traded away to obtain a roller coaster ride. With B = 4, Ph = 1, and Pr = 1 all five possible choices of R and H lie along the budget constraint line beginning at the R axis intercept of 4R,0H.

In figure 1.3 the indifference curves have been drawn so that the optimal choices that occurred with cardinal or measurable utility will correspond to the optimal choices in which ordinal utility ranking is assumed. Other than the price of roller coaster rides (Pr) all factors such as income, prices of other goods, and tastes and preferences are assumed to be the same. Since the optimal choices are the same as before, plotting the optimal choice quantities of roller coaster rides (R) against the two prices Pr = 2 and Pr = 1 will generate the same downward sloping demand curve as D_1 as in figure 1.1. That is, for Pr = 2, Qr = 1 and for Pr = 1, Qr = 2.

Cardinal and ordinal utilities have different advantages when illustrating consumer demand. One of the biggest advantages from assuming measurable or cardinal utility is that diminishing marginal utility along a given demand curve is observable. Observable marginal utilities make it easier to illustrate the concept of rational choice in terms of choice consequences (benefits and costs). For a given good such as roller-coaster rides (R), a rational choice (assuming the objective is utility maximization) can be determined by comparing price (marginal cost) to demand (marginal utility or benefit) for the next unit of (R) consumed. A choice is rational and the consumer has the opportunity to become better off through consumption of the next unit of good (R) if the demand curve is greater than the price. The concept of diminishing marginal utility is particularly important when illustrating rational choice and when measuring public sector demand.

Ordinal utility, on the other hand, is convenient for illustrating the income and substitution effects associated with a price change. Income and substitution effects are important to understand because they illustrate that different forces may influence consumer behavior. (That different forces may influence rational actions/choices is very important when analyzing murder as a business decision.)

The income and substitution effects of a change in Pr are illustrated in figure 1.4. The influence of the income and substitution effect of a change in price such as Pr = 2 to Pr = 1 actually decomposes the consumer's behavioral responses to the price change into two components. One response component is that the decrease in Pr will cause the consumer to substitute relatively more roller coaster rides (R) and fewer hamburgers (H) into consumption, all else, including the income effect, held constant. This is the substitution effect of the ΔPr (the symbol "Δ" means "change in"). The substitution effect represents a new optimal choice bundle of goods R and H and is represented by a movement along a given indifference curve that occurs in response to a change in the price ratios of the two goods. Now, given the substitution effect, the other response component is that the decrease in Pr will allow the consumer to buy more units of both goods R and

II. This is the income effect of a ΔPr and it is what leads to an increase in total utility or benefits consumed (i.e., the move to a higher indifference curve).

To summarize, a ΔPr → ΔQr (that is, a change in Pr leads to a change in Qr) in the opposite direction, all else held constant. The behavior response to a ΔPr is a ΔQr that consists of two separate components. One is the substitution or "price-ratio" effect and the other is the income or "total utility" effect.

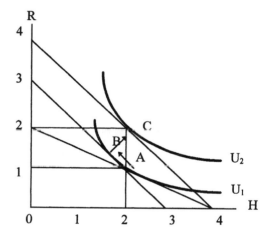

Fig. 1.4. Substitution and Income Effects. Substitution effects illustrate the tendency to buy more of the relatively cheaper good as the price ratio changes. The change in the price ratio -Ph/Pr (i.e., the slope of the budget line) is represented by a rotation of the budget line to the new price ratio -Ph/Pr and new slope while remaining tangent to the original indifference curve. Specifically, decreasing Pr = 2 to Pr = 1 results in an increase in the price ratio from -1/2 to -1/1. Because good R has become cheaper relative to good H, the consumer substitutes relatively more R and less H into consumption by moving from A to B on indifference curve U₁. The income effect from a price decrease allows the consumer to achieve a higher level of total utility. The income effect from the same price decrease is illustrated by a movement away from the origin from point B on U₁ to point C on U₂. At the new price ratios the budget line shifts outward and away from the origin. The new R axis intercept is given by B/Pr = 4/1 = 4.

The income and substitution effects cannot be clearly delineated in the cardinal utility example in which the consumer first chooses 1R,2H at Pr = 2 and then chooses 2R,2H at Pr = 1. It simply appears that the consumer substituted relatively more roller coaster rides (R) into consumption, suggesting that only the substitution effect is present. However, the observed increase in total utility (an increase in utils) does allow for the inference of an income effect. On the other hand, the indifference curves and budget constraints of figure 1.4 make it possible to observe both the income and substitution effects separately. Figure 1.4 shows the income and substitution effects that result from a decrease in Pr = 2 to Pr = 1 using the same set of indifference curves and budget constraints as in figure 1.3.

The substitution effect is really a price ratio effect that occurs while holding all else (including the income effect) constant. Thus while the consumer is still at the same level of utility on indifference curve U_1 the increase in the price ratios from -Ph/Pr = -1/2 to -Ph/Pr = -1/1 causes the consumer to substitute away from the now relatively higher priced good (H) and toward the now relatively lower priced good (R). In figure 1.4 the substitution effect is illustrated by the movement away from the H axis and toward the R axis or, more specifically, from optimal choice A to optimal choice B on U_1.

In figure 1.4 only the income effect of a price change causes an increasing change in the index of total utility from U_1 to U_2. The increase in total utility is illustrated by the outward shift in the budget constraint line (at the new price ratios) in which the consumer moves from optimal choice B to optimal choice C. The decrease in Pr = 2 to Pr = 1, all else (including the substitution effect) held constant, allows the consumer to buy more of both goods R and H or, equivalently, more total utility or benefits with fixed budget resources (B). Assuming that the consumer gains positive marginal utility from the consumption of both goods R and H, the increase in total utility will be indicated by a movement that is generally away from the origin.

The income and substitution effects are simply two different forces that cause predictable changes in consumer behavior. In terms of the demand curve derived from the two prices and optimal quantities of R consumed figure 1.5 indicates that part of the increasing change in the quantity demanded of good R is due to the substitution effect (S) and the other part is due to the income effect (I).

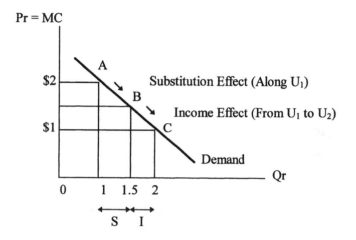

Fig. 1.5. Demand for Roller-Coaster Rides. The substitution effect S explains the movement along the demand curve from A to B and corresponds to the movement along indifference curve U_1 in figure 1.4. The Income effect (I) explains the movement along the demand curve from B to C and corresponds to the movement from indifference curve U_1 to indifference curve U_2. The consumer is changing his or her behavior (i.e., changing quantity demanded) due to the degree that each of these two forces effect rational choices. Although it may appear to be the case, the degree to which either of the two forces (S and I) influence consumer behavior need not be the same.

Substitution and income effects may not influence consumer behavior or quantity demanded equally. This is because the particular characteristics of a good may cause the consumer to relate to it in different ways in response to a change in its price. For example, a relatively low priced item that is characterized by many close substitutes in consumption (such as chicken soup) is likely to have a relatively large substitution effect associated with even very small relative price changes. For low priced items that do not constitute a major aspect of the consumer's budget expenditures the price change will also generate a relatively modest income or total utility effect. On the other hand, big ticket items that constitute a major aspect of the consumer's budget expenditures (such as transportation and shelter) will tend to exhibit much larger income or total utility effects when their prices change. Generally, the income effect will explain the greatest proportion of the change in consumer behavior (i.e., change in consumer demand) for big ticket items. On the other hand the price ratio or substitution effect may be relatively less significant if there are few substitutes available.

ELASTICITIES

Elasticities are quantitative measures of the relative sensitivity of consumer behavior (i.e., demand) to a change in particular decision parameters such as price, income, or the price of another related good. Elasticities are important to murder as a business decision because it will be shown that homicide offender responses to particular decision parameters can also be assessed.

Price elasticities are the most common type of elasticity measures. A price elasticity measures the extent of a change in quantity demanded that occurs in response to a change in the price of that good or service, all else held constant. Price elasticities consist of the percentage change in the quantity demand (%ΔQ) divided by the percentage change in price (%ΔP). A commonly used formula for the price elasticity of demand at some point (P*, Q*) on a linear demand curve (given by $Q = a - bP$) can be derived directly from the definition of price elasticities. Letting $e_{Q,P}$ denote the elasticity of Q with respect to P we have,

$$e_{Q,P} = \text{(Percentage change in Q*)/(Percentage change in P*)} \qquad (1.3)$$
$$= (\Delta Q/Q*)/(\Delta P/P*)$$
$$= (\Delta Q/\Delta P) \times (P*/Q*).$$

The resulting price elasticity $e_{Q,P}$ is expected to be negative because of the assumed inverse relationship between P and Q on a given demand curve.

Since the slope of a linear demand curve is given by $-b = \Delta Q/\Delta P$ equation (1.3) can be written as

$$e_{Q,P} = (\Delta Q/\Delta P) \times (P*/Q*) \qquad (1.4)$$
$$= -b \times P*/Q*.$$

Equation (1.4) shows the $e_{Q,P}$ is not constant on a linear demand curve. That is, as the ratio $P*/Q*$ increases, so to will the value of the point elasticity of demand. This holds true for all but the most extreme cases of horizontal (perfectly elastic) or vertical (perfectly inelastic) demand curves. In order to make the measured point elasticity of demand as relevant to the decision maker as possible, $P*$ and $Q*$ are usually the mean values of the market observations.

In some cases, demand curves are assumed to be linear in the logarithms of Q and P. When this is so the demand equation is written as

$$\log Q = a - b \log P. \qquad (1.5)$$

In this case the price elasticity of demand is given by $-b$ and is the same at every point on the non-linear (i.e., log linear) demand curve.

The effect of changes in other decision parameters such as consumer incomes and the prices of other goods can be measured by other types of elasticities. All elasticity measures have the causal force (such as $\%\Delta P$) as the denominator and the resulting behavioral change (such as $\%\Delta Q$) as the numerator. Since elasticities are measured as ratios, an absolute value that is greater than one indicates a response that is "elastic" or highly sensitive to a change in a particular decision parameter. In contrast, an elasticity ratio with an absolute value less than one indicates an "inelastic" or insensitive responsive. If a measured elasticity has an absolute value of one then it indicates "unit elasticity,"

As indicated, price elasticities are always negative. This is why they are sometimes expressed as absolute values. For income and cross-price elasticities the direction of effect is more important and absolute values are not used. In terms of a given demand curve, a price elasticity holds the demand curve in place (i.e., all else is assumed to be held constant) while changes in income or the prices of other goods cause the demand curve to shift horizontally to the left or right (that is, change the level of demand).

An income elasticity is a measure of the relationship between consumer income and the level of demand for a particular good or service. If the income elasticity is positive and less than or equal to unity the good is defined to be normal (e.g., pizza), if it is positive and greater than unity the good is defined as a luxury (e.g., private school). If the income elasticity is negative the good is defined as inferior (e.g., moonshine).

Cross-price elasticities are measures of the relationship between another good's price and the level of demand for a given good or service. If a cross-price elasticity is positive both goods are considered to be substitutes (e.g., tea and coffee). If a cross-price elasticity is negative both goods are considered to be complements (e.g., bread and butter).

SUGGESTED READINGS

1. Battalio, et. al., "A Test of Consumer Demand Theory Using Observations of Individual Purchases," *Western Economic Journal* (December 1973): 411-428.

CHAPTER 2

PRODUCER CHOICE THEORY

In this chapter a simple short-run production process is developed from which optimal output choices can be determined. The concept of production or, equivalently, cost efficiency is also developed and is discussed in terms of both short-run and long-run production processes. It will become apparent that the analysis of producer and consumer choice have a great number of similarities. These similarities are emphasized for pedagogical purposes. A brief discussion of statistical probabilities is included at the end of the chapter. Understanding statistical probabilities is important in the chapters that follow.

SIMILARITIES IN CONSUMPTION AND PRODUCTION

Recall that in the consumer model of Chapter 1 price served as a the marginal cost of the next unit consumed. With perfect information assumed, the inversely related P,Q pairs that lie along the consumer's demand curve represented optimal utility maximizing consumer choices. Thus price, when expressed in terms of the consumer's demand curve and rational consumer choice, actually became a deterrent or disincentive to the action choice of consumption at the point where price (marginal cost) began to exceed the marginal utility (benefit) reflected in the consumer's downward sloping demand curve. Given a consumer's budget resources, the income effect of a price change also determined the maximum level of utility to be gained through the act of consumption. In other words, when price increased, total utility (benefit) decreased along with the amount consumed.

The producer choice model is very similar to the model of consumer choice except that price plays the role of an incentive to producer action as opposed to a disincentive or deterrent role. From the producer's point of view, price serves as the marginal benefit to the activity of production. Increases in the price of output are, therefore, expected to entice an increase in the quantity of production. The incentive effect of price suggests that supply curves should slope up and to the right when the quantity of output is plotted against price. Increases in price and quantity supplied also increase the producer's total revenue or benefit.

Another reason that supply curves slope upwards is that in the short-run, when the quantity of at least one factor of production is fixed (such as plant size), the diminishing marginal product of the variable factor (such as labor) as it is added to the fixed factor will increase per unit production costs at the margin. Supply curves represent increasing marginal costs (or, equivalently, diminishing marginal product the variable factor) and must, therefore, slope upwards. Diminishing marginal utility in demand is analogous to diminishing marginal product in supply.

Profit maximization is the assumed objective of the producer and is conceptually similar to the consumer's assumed objective of utility maximization. In fact, one could argue that both objectives are really the same thing. Both objectives suggest that individual resource owners simply want to maximize the returns to their scarce resources. Like utility maximization, profit maximization is broadly applicable.

As in the consumer model in which assumed rational consumers increased purchases (and total utility) only if MB ≥ MC (that is, MU ≥ price), assumed rational producers will increase production (and total profits) only if MR > MC (that is, price ≥ MC). Assuming perfect information, the positively related P,Q pairs that lie along an upward sloping supply curve are the result of optimal profit maximizing producer choices.

Other similarities between consumer and producer choice models are that the indifference curves of the constrained utility-maximization consumer model appear as isoquants in the producer model. Both indifference curves and isoquants represent an index level. Indifference curves are indexes of the level of utility for equally preferred bundles of goods and isoquants are measurable levels of output. The budget constraints of the consumer model are cost constraints in the producer model. In both the consumer and producer models the constraints (budget or cost) represent the maximum level of utility or output attainable. In some cases, however, the total cost constraints of the producer model may be bowed outward as opposed to being linear.

A SHORT-RUN PRODUCTION PROCESS

At first let us limit our concern to the period of time known as the short-run. By definition the short-run is any period of time in which the quantity of at least one factor of production (such as plant size or land) is fixed. In contrast, the long-run is any period of time in which the quantities of all factors of production are variable. The short-run may be a longer period of time for a more capital intensive production process. Capital intensive production processes involve a higher proportion of machines and production facilities that cannot be easily varied. An example would be a nuclear power plant. On the other hand, a labor intensive production process uses factors or production (such as workers) that may be more easily varied. An example would be a police unit. If the capital equipment used in labor intensive production processes can be easily varied then the short-run may be a relatively short period of time.

A garbage collection service will serve as an adequate example of a short-run production process. In this example it is assumed that there is just one garbage truck and that there are different numbers of equally capable workers assigned to it. Since there is only one garbage truck the garbage truck serves as the fixed factor of production in the short-run. In effect, the garbage truck can be considered as simply one fixed unit of capital equipment. Let the variable K_c represent the number of units of capital equipment (that is, garbage trucks) where the "c" indicates that "K" is a fixed factor. The number of equally capable workers per hour assigned to the garbage truck can be represented by the variable L where L stands for the number of units of labor. When L represents the number of workers per hour L is equivalent to the number of man-hours used per hour. Thus one unit of L equals one man-hour or one worker per hour. As in most real world production process's labor (L) is the most important short-run variable input. Let output (Q) be the quantity of trash cans collected and dumped per hour.

It is important to note that the variables Q, L, and K_c are measured in units per period of time. In this example the period of time is one hour. This means that these variables can be stated either as units of occurrence or as rates of occurrence.

Increases in units of labor (L) assigned to the fixed factor K_c should provide some opportunity for specialization in the production process. For example, if only one worker is assigned to the garbage truck, he or she would have to do all tasks such as driving and dumping trash cans. However, two workers can specialize. One can drive while the other collects and dumps the trash cans. Compared with one worker, specialization would eliminate some repetitive tasks such as stopping, parking, getting in and out of the truck, and walking around the truck. The effect of specialization will substantially increase the number of units of output (Q) produced by the production process in a given period of time. In fact, because some repetitive tasks are reduced or eliminated, the change in the rate or number of units of output (Q) should be greater than the change in the rate or number of units of labor. In other words, doubling the units of labor L should result in more than a doubling in Q because of the effect of specialization.

Output (Q) per unit of the next factor input (measured by holding all other factors or inputs constant) is the marginal product of that factor.[1] For labor (L) this would be the marginal product of labor or MPL. If, due to specialization, the change in the rate or number of units of output (Q) is greater than the change in the rate or number of units of labor (L), then MPL must be greater for the second worker. Unfortunately, as more and more workers are assigned to the fixed factor K_c (the garbage truck) opportunities to specialize and eliminate repetitive tasks are likely to become less and less. For example, a third worker could walk ahead of the truck and open or rearrange trash cans to facilitate dumping. However, a fourth worker may only be able to contribute directly to the redundant task of collecting and dumping trash cans. Thus as workers continue to be added to a production process that has a fixed factor such as K_c increases in output (Q) per unit of the variable factor L will begin to increase by diminishing amounts. In other words, beyond some point the effects of specialization in the use of labor will begin to diminish and, correspondingly, the marginal product of labor (MPL) will also begin to diminish.

The limited opportunities in specialization mean that each successive worker finds that, no matter how hard he or she works, they are physically able to contribute fewer and fewer units of output (Q) to the production process. Regardless of the workers' intentions, it is even possible that increases in the rate of output (Q) per unit of variable factor input (that is, the marginal product of labor) could even become negative beyond some point. In the garbage dumping example a negative MPL could happen if the number of workers assigned to the garbage truck become so many (perhaps more than four or five) that they begin to get into each other's way and slowing the production process. It is generally true, for any short-run production process, that continued increases in the rate of utilization of a variable factor will, beyond some point, cause the rate of output to begin to increase by diminishing amounts.

It is expected that producers will always add units of labor (L) when specialization creates increasing MPL. It is also expected that producers will not add workers beyond the point where MPL becomes negative.

Once the marginal cost of labor (L) is considered, optimal allocations of labor (L) to fixed capital K_c (tend to occur somewhere in the range of positive but diminishing MPL. This is illustrated in the following example. Let the wage rate be w = $10.00 per hour and assume that there are no additional non-monetary benefits given to workers. The marginal cost of each unit of labor (L) is then MCL = w = $10.00 per hour. Moreover, since output (Q) varies directly with labor (L) when MPL is positive, the marginal cost of output (Q) is directly related to w or MCL. Accordingly, the marginal cost of output (Q) is calculated simply as MC = MCL/MPL = w/MPL. In other words, the marginal cost (MC) of the increased output (Q) must be the cost of the worker w (w is the cost of the increased output) divided by change in the units of output or MPL. Since w is assumed fixed the MC of output (Q) increases as MPL diminishes. The production process should continue to add labor L to fixed factor K_c (that is, increase output Q) as long as the marginal benefit of output is greater than or equal to the marginal cost of output. The price of output is the marginal benefit (or revenue) to the producer so the short-run production process should expand L and Q to the point at which price (marginal revenue) equals the increasing marginal output cost (MC). Thus profits are maximized when price (P) or marginal revenue (MR) is equal to marginal cost (MC).

Table 2.1 provides a summary of the relationship between output (Q) and the variable factor (L) for the garbage dumping example. The marginal product of labor MPL and the marginal cost of different levels of output (assuming that w = $10.00) are also provided. Setting the price of output P = $0.20 = marginal revenue (MR), optimization or profit maximization at MR = MC occurs when L* = 4 workers per hour and Q* = 290 cans dumped per hour. Referring to the MPL column in table 2.1 it is clearly indicated that optimization occurs in the diminishing range of MPL. This is important because diminishing MPL causes increasing MC and increasing MC represents the producer's short-run supply curve.

Table 2.1

Garbage Truck Production Process

Cans Dumped (Q) Per Hour	Workers (L) Per Hour	Garbage Trucks (K_c) Per Hour	Marginal Product of Labor (MPL $= \Delta Q/\Delta L$)	Marginal Cost of Production (MC $=$ w/MPL)
0	0	1		
60	1	1	60	$10/60 = $0.167
160	2	1	100	$10/100 = $0.10
240	3	1	80	$10/80 = $0.125
290 *	4 *	1	50	$10/50 = $0.20
310	5	1	20	$10/20 = $0.50

Note: The optimal output level or rate Q* and the optimal number or rate of labor L* utilized occurs at the point when MR = MC = $0.20. Notice that this occurs in the range where MPL is diminishing.

Production and Cost Functions

Perfect information allows the assumed rational producer to choose the optimal or profit maximizing levels or rates of output Q* and input L*. To the producer perfect information means that the marginal benefit (revenue) and marginal cost of each output choice Q is known with certainty. For a trash collection service, the unit price or MR can be determined by taking each homeowner's monthly trash bill and dividing it by the number of trash cans dumped each month. For example, assuming that each homeowner's monthly trash collection bill is $1.60 and that each homeowner has one can of trash to dump and that the trash is dumped twice each week (eight times each month) the unit price, marginal revenue (MR), and average revenue to the producer would be exactly \$0.20. If the price of each unit of output (Q) is fixed as in this example, then marginal revenue (MR) always equals the price (P) and the average revenue (AR) that the producer receives for each and every unit of production. If the price or marginal revenue (MR) is not fixed then average revenue (AR) is always less than MR and the optimal output level (Q) is a bit more difficult to determine. In any case, marginal revenue (MR) is always defined to be the change in total revenue (TR) divided by the change in output (Q) or $MR = \Delta TR / \Delta Q$.

The far right column of table 2.1 provides the marginal cost information required for the producer to determine the optimal output choice Q*. In table 2.1 the marginal cost of output (MC) is calculated as $MC = w/MPL$. Even if w is fixed, the variation in MPL will cause a MC to also vary. More specifically, the variation of MC is always inversely related to the direction of variation in MPL. It should be pointed out that by definition the marginal cost of output (MC) can also be calculated as the change in total cost divided by the change in output Q. In other words, $MC = \Delta TC / \Delta Q = w/MPL$. This is because in the short-run ΔTC is due only to $\Delta MCL = w$ and ΔQ is always equal to MPL.

To the producer the marginal benefit and marginal cost (that is, the consequences) of each output choice (Q) in table 2.1 are known with perfect certainty. The producer increases profit by increasing the output level or rate of output (Q) as long as the marginal revenue (MR) of each can of trash dumped is greater than or equal to the marginal cost (MC) of dumping it. When the level or rate of output (Q) increases to where marginal cost (MC) exceeds marginal revenue (MR) it is no longer in the producers interest to increase the rate of production. This is the "irrational zone" of production. The marginal product of labor (MPL) may still be positive but be at such a low value that it causes marginal cost (MC) to become vary high. In the irrational zone, increases in the rate or level of production cause the producer to move farther and farther away from his/her assumed goal of profit maximization. It follows that the optimal rate or level of production (Q*) is exactly at the point where marginal revenue (MR) just equals marginal cost (MC).

The optimal rate or level of output (Q* = 290) is illustrated graphically in figure 2.1A as the intersection of marginal cost (MC) and marginal revenue (MR). Together, figure 2.1A and 2.1B provide a graphical illustration of optimal output (Q*) and the associated optimal labor input (L*). Figure 2.1A also illustrates the short-run supply or marginal cost curve that slopes up and to the right. The supply curve is the marginal cost curve because the optimal output choice (Q*) always occurs at the point when MR = MC. Thus changes in price or marginal revenue (MR) will map out a whole set of positively related P,Q* pairs that lie along the marginal cost (MC) curve.

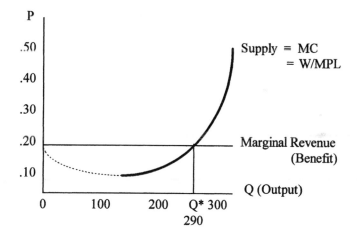

Fig. 2.1A. Short-Run Supply Curve or Marginal Cost Function. When MR or price ($0.20) exceeds MC for the next higher level or rate of output, total profits can be increased by increasing output (Q). When MC exceeds MR an increase in Q will decrease profits. Thus the optimal profit maximizing rate or level of output (Q*) occurs at the point where MR = MC = $0.20. In this example Q* - 290 cans dumped per hour.

The production function in figure 2.1B is simply a graphical summary of the relationship between output (Q) and inputs (L and K). In the short-run the production function summarizes the relationship between the variable input (L) and output (Q) while holding the units of capital, the one garbage truck, (K_c) constant. The optimal output of $Q^* = 290$ occurs when $L^* = 4$ workers per hour. The marginal product of a worker or man-hour (MPL) is equal to the slope of the production function at that number of workers. The decreasing change in the slope of the production function that begins to occur at $L = 2$ workers indicates diminishing marginal product of labor (MPL). Because MPL is given by the slope of the production function at each unit of labor (L), the production function and marginal cost (or supply curves) are mathematically related.

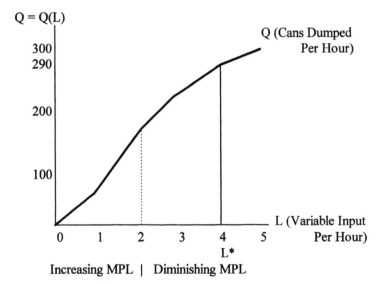

Fig. 2.1B. Labor Production Function. The optimal output Q^* and variable input L^* correspond to each other because the production function in 2.1B is mathematically related to the marginal cost (supply) curve in 2.1A.

Optimal Output and Production Efficiency

Figure 2.1a and 2.1b indicate that the optimal output choice O* = 290 corresponds to an optimal variable input choice of L* = 4 workers per hour assigned to the garbage truck. Thus the optimal output choice requires that the producer also assign an optimal amount of the variable factor (L) to the fixed factor (K_c). The mathematical relationship between the optimal output Q* and optimal variable resource allocation L* can be shown as follows:

$$MR = MC \text{ at } Q^* \quad \text{(Optimal rate of Output)} \qquad (2.1a)$$

by substitution,

$$P = w/MPL \qquad (2.1b)$$

$$P \times MPL = w \qquad (2.1c)$$

$$MRP = MCL \text{ at } L^* \text{ (Optimal L Allocation).} \qquad (2.1d)$$

In equation (2.1d) MRP is the marginal revenue product of labor. MRP is calculated as $P \times MPL = MRP$ and is the marginal benefit (MBL) of each worker to the producer. The marginal benefit of labor consists of each unit of L's incremental physical contribution to output (MPL) multiplied by the price or marginal revenue of each unit of the incremental output (P). That is, MBL = MRP = P × MPL. The MRP or MBL diminishes due to diminishing MPL. Thus the MRP is the producers downward sloping demand (or marginal benefit) curve for labor (L).

Since marginal revenue product (MRP) is the diminishing marginal benefit curve of labor to a producer and serves as the producers demand for labor, the demand for labor is similar to the demand for consumer goods and services. For consumers it was assumed that diminishing marginal utility (benefit) generated a negatively sloped consumer demand curve. For labor demand the diminishing marginal benefit of labor MRP = P × MPL also generates a down sloping labor demand curve. Even with price (P) fixed, MRP will still slope downward or diminish because of the diminishing value of MPL. The producer's demand curve for labor is illustrated in figure 2.2.

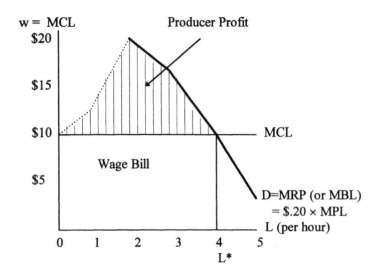

Fig. 2.2. The Producer's Demand for Labor. The labor demand curve D is derived from the price of output ($0.20) and the diminishing MPL of each unit of L that begins to occur at 2 workers. The optimal level or rate of the variable factor L assigned to the fixed factor K_c occures at L* = 4 workers per hour and represents a rational choice in the context of the assumed profit maximizing objective. The area under the MRP curve is the total returns to all factors of production. Total returns can be subdivided into returns to the owner (producer profit) and returns to labor (wage bill).

Only those units of labor (L) in which the marginal benefit to the producer (MRP) is greater than or equal to the marginal cost of labor (w) will contribute towards profit maximization and, hence, will be hired by a rational producer. In other words, the rational profit maximizing producer hires a worker only if that worker can make the producer money. When MBL ≤ MCL too many workers have been hired and the producer loses money or profits on those workers. Given that the marginal cost of labor MCL = w = $10.00 per hour, the optimal profit maximizing number of workers must be L* = 4 where MRP = MCL = $10.00.

In figure 2.2 the portion of the labor demand curve in which MBL ≥ MCL is the return or profit to the producer. These accounting profits are really just the return to the owner or producer as a resource and must be paid if the business is going to continue to exist. In terms of rational producer choice, if profits are not paid (or are significantly taxed away) the optimal level of capital (K) may become zero. Moreover, if capital (K) is zero, the optimal level of labor (L) will very likely also be zero.

In the short-run the optimal level or rate of output (Q*) that maximizes profits may or may not be the minimum cost level of output. In general terms, economic efficiency means to achieve a goal with the least cost. In more specific terms, production efficiency means to minimize costs for any given level of output (Q) produced or, equivalently, to maximize output (Q) for any given level of costs.

A level of output (Q) can be related to the inputs of capital (K) and labor (L) graphically as an isoquant. All points on an isoquant are assumed to be technically efficient. Technical efficiency in production refers to processes that produce a given level of output with the least amount of inputs. In other words, the best known technology is being used. Technical efficiency is reflected by a negatively sloped and convex isoquant where a producer cannot reduce the usage of one input and keep output the same without increasing the usage of one or more other inputs. By assumption, if the best technology is not used, then production does not occur on an isoquant. This means that minimum cost production or production efficiency can never be achieved. In other words, technical efficiency is required before production efficiency is possible. Given the factor prices and a convex isoquant, only one technically efficient process will also reflect production (cost) efficiency or minimum costs.

In the model of producer choice variations in output price will cause the mathematically related variables MR and MRP to vary. Holding resource prices and technology constant, variations in MR and MRP will cause the producer to increase or decrease the profit maximizing output level (Q*). In the short-run, variations in output (Q) must either increase or decrease the level of labor (L) relative to the fixed level of capital (K). Even though all combinations of K and L on a given isoquant are assumed to be technically efficient, the particular combination of L and K necessary to produce a given Q* may not achieve production efficiency.

Figure 2.3 illustrates the short-run production (or cost) efficiency problem. In figure 2.3 the production isoquant Q_{290} (the profit maximizing rate of output) shows all combinations of K and L that the producer is able to use in order to keep the level of output constant at Q = 290. In addition to the assumption of technical efficiency, production isoquants rely on a rationale similar to that of indifference curves in order to explain their convex shape. Along any isoquant in figure 2.3 it is assumed that increasing uses of a factor of production contribute positively, yet marginally less and less, to output. This means that these isoquants will have no flat spots so that a unique solution occurs. The total cost of a given level of production in figure 2.3 is represented by straight lines that are analogous to a consumer's budget constraint. The total cost curves are developed mathematically by letting (w) equal the price of labor and (v) equal the price of capital. Thus the total cost (TC) of a given level of output (Q) produced by inputs of L and K is given by equation (2.2) such that,

$$TC = wL + vK. \tag{2.2}$$

By solving for K and re-arranging the terms equation (2.2) can be re-written as

$$K = (TC/v) - (w/vL). \tag{2.3}$$

Equation (2.3) is the familiar linear slope-intercept equation for the total cost constraints where TC/v is the K axis intercept and - w/vL is the slope.

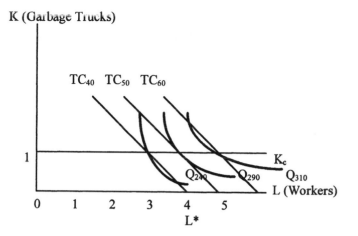

Fig. 2.3. Optimal and Efficient Input Choice. At L* = 4 and Q* = 290, the isoquant Q_{290} just touches the total cost constraint TC_{50}. This point of tangency reflects an optimal and productively efficient input/output choice in which profit is maximized at the same time that output is maximized at a given level of cost or, equivalently, that cost is minimized for a given level of output. A higher or lower number of workers (L) assigned to fixed factor K_c (that is, any other level of technically efficient production) will result in a loss of production or cost efficiency. This is indicated by the isoquants not being tangent to the cost constraints at that level of production.

For convenience it can be assumed that the garbage truck rents for $10.00 per hour, including the cost of gasoline. Since w = $10.00 per hour we also have w = v = $10.00 per hour. According to equation (2.3) the total cost (TC) constraints have a negative slope of -w/v = -$10/$10 = -1 and the K axis intercept given by TC/v = TC/$10. Assuming that MPL and MPK remain positive total cost (TC) varies directly with the level of output (Q). At the optimal input/output combination of Q* = 290, L* = 4, and K_c = 1, total cost (TC) can be calculated as TC = $10(4) + $10(1) = 50.00 per hour ($TC_{50}$). Total revenue (TR) can be calculated at Q* as TR = P × Q* = $.20 × 290 = $58.00. At the optimal rate of output (Q*) total revenue minus total cost is TR - TC = $58 - $50 = $8.00. Therefore, $8.00 must be the maximum attainable accounting profit per hour.

In figure 2.3, production or cost efficiency can be seen to occur only when the production isoquants are just tangent to the total cost curves. It is assumed that production efficiency occurs at output level $Q* = 290$ (and input level $L* = 4$ and $K_c = 1$) where TC_{50} is just tangent to Q_{290}. At this point of tangency, output is maximized ($Q* = 290$) for a given level of resources (TC_{50}). Equivalently, cost is minimized (TC_{50}) for a given level of output ($Q* = 290$). Although they are assumed technically efficient, all other isoquants and corresponding TC constraints do not exhibit production efficiency because the isoquants are inside the total cost curves at some point. For all other levels of production it would be possible to move to the surface of the total cost constraint and increase the level of production if both inputs K_c and L were variable. Stated differently, if both K_c and L were variable total costs could be reduced for some levels of production. Thus even though technical efficiency and profit maximization are always assumed, production (cost) efficiency or minimum cost production may not occur in the short-run.

Figure 2.3 provides another way of looking at short-run production or cost inefficiency. To the left of $Q*,L*$ production is inefficient because too few workers (L) are assigned to fixed capital (K_c). To the right of $Q*,L*$ production is inefficient because there are too many workers (L) are assigned to fixed capital (K_c). In the long-run, when all resources are variable, both technical and production (cost) efficiency should correspond to all profit maximizing levels or rates of output (Q).

It is also useful to consider that production (cost) efficiency can be stated in the same way as the consumer's utility maximization criterion. Consumer utility is maximized when per dollar marginal utilities or "bang-for-the-buck" for all goods consumed is equalized when the consumer's budget is exhausted. For production or cost efficiency, the rate of technical substitution (RTS) of labor L for capital K along any isoquant Q_n must be equal to the price ratios of the two factors (i.e., the slope of the TC constraint) at the point of tangency with the corresponding TC constraint. By definition, the RTS of L for K is always equal to the ratios of the marginal products of the two factors (MPL and MPK). For simplicity, assume that MPK = MPL = 50 at the tangency condition at Q_{290} and TC_{50} in figure 2.3. From the example it is also known that w = v = \$10. Thus at the point of tangency

$$- (MPL/MPK) = - (w/v) \qquad (2.4)$$

By substitution,

$$- (50/50) = - (10/10)$$

or,

$$-1 = -1.$$

After rearranging equation (2.4) we have

$$MPL/w = MPK/v \qquad (2.5)$$

By substitution,

$$50/10 = 50/10$$

or,

$$5 = 5.$$

The tangency condition indicated in figure 2.3 and by equation (2.5) means that the producers "bang-for-the-buck" is equalized for a given level of producer costs. For both producers and consumers this means that output or utility, respectively, is maximized for a given level of expenditures.

As resource owners' producers and consumers are simply making decisions that allocate their scarce resources in such a way as to gain the highest returns possible. It should not be too surprising that the mathematical re-statement of these conditions for producers and consumers should also look the same. Regardless of whether the returns sought by resource owners are measurable (such as profits) or subjective (such as utility) it is always true that economic behavior is equivalent to efficient behavior.

PRODUCTION EFFICIENCY IN THE LONG-RUN

In the long-run all resources or factors of production are variable. This includes the quantity of plant and equipment or capital (K). In the garbage dumping example this means that more garbage trucks could be added to the production process. Variable capital also means that, in addition to changes in a given firm's plant and equipment, firms may enter and leave an industry. The variability of all factors of production in the long-run raises many additional issues. New issues discussed include returns to scale and technological progress. Other issues to be discussed are also relevant to the short-run and include changes in factor prices and economic profits.

The term "returns to scale" refers to the rate at which output increases in response to a proportional increase in all factors including plant size and the amount of capital equipment. For example, if the increase in output is less than the proportionate increase in inputs there are decreasing returns to scale (or diseconomies of scale). Decreasing returns to scale may be due to information loss, duplication of effort, loss of management control, and a lack of management direction. These problems tend to become worse when the scale of production increases to very large sizes. In contrast to decreasing returns to scale, increasing returns to scale (or economies of scale) occur when output increases proportionately more than an increase in all inputs. In the long-run increasing returns to scale are due to increased specialization and, as in the short-run, tend to occur more significantly during the initial stages of output expansion. If output doubles when all inputs are doubled there are constant returns to scale. Constant returns to scale reflect the offsetting forces of economies and diseconomies of scale.

Long-run returns to scale are illustrated by the segmented per-unit average cost curve LAC_0 in figure 2.4 and by the three associated production isoquant maps in figure 2.5. In the long-run all firms in the industry are expected to produce at least as much output as that which corresponds to the minimum efficient scale (MES) of operation. This is because any firm producing in the decreasing returns range or at less than the minimum efficient scale (MES) would have higher costs than other competing firms and must expand its scale of operations or be driven out of business.

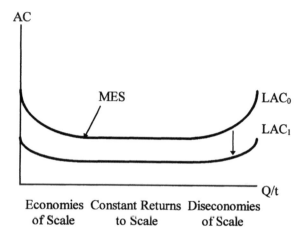

Fig. 2.4. Returns to Scale and the Long-Run Per-Unit Average Cost Curve

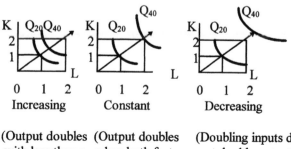

Fig. 2.5. Returns to Scale and Production Isoquant Maps

Changes in technology and factor prices also effect per unit costs. For example, if one or both factor prices decrease, per unit costs will decrease and the LAC will shift downward such as from LAC_0 to LAC_1 in figure 2.4. Holding factor prices constant, a neutral or unbiased improvement in technology (that is, an improvement that effects the productivity of labor and capital equally) will increase returns to any scale of operations. This will also shift per unit costs and the long-run average cost curve downward such as from LAC_0 to LAC_1. Because changes in technology and factor prices shift the entire cost function (such as LAC) the factor prices and technology associated with any given cost function are assumed to be held constant. Thus changes in factor prices and technology do not explain differences in the returns to scale for a given cost function. This is just like a consumer demand curve. All factors that would shift a cost or supply function must also be held constant when talking about movements along it.

Competition provides a powerful incentive to control factor costs and to enhance factor productivity through the research, development, and implementation of better technologies. In other words, competition not only results in MES operations it results in the lowest LAC possible. Moreover, since all resources are variable in the long-run production efficiency is assured.

The distinction between economic and accounting profit is another important issue. Accounting profit is defined to be the difference between total revenue (TR) and total accounting costs (TC). Accounting costs are payments or returns to the or non-owner resources of the firm. If total revenue (TR) and total accounting costs (TC) are each divided by output quantity (Q) the result is average revenue (AR) and average accounting costs (AC or LAC). Accounting profit is then the difference between average revenue (AR) and average accounting costs (LAC). Moreover, since total revenue (TR) is price (P) multiplied by quantity (TR = P × Q), average revenue (AR) must also equal output price (that is, AR = TR/Q = P). Also, if output price (P) is constant over the range of output or sales, then price is equal to average revenue (AR) and marginal revenue (that is, AR = P = MR). Regardless of whether price (P) is fixed, the profit maximizing rate of output production (Q*) in both the long-run and the short-run is always at the point where marginal revenue (MR) equals marginal costs (MC or LMC).

If price (P) is fixed and, therefore, equal to average revenue (AR) and marginal revenue (MR) and long-run average cost (LAC) is equal to average per-unit accounting costs (that is, TC/Q = LAC), then accounting profit can be determined graphically as in figure 2.6.

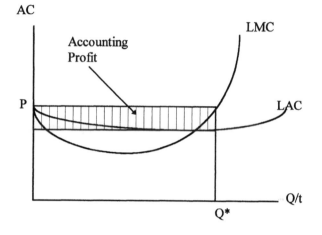

Fig. 2.6. Long-Run Profit Maximization. LAC is long-run average cost and LMC is long-run marginal cost. The profit maximizing rate of output Q* occurs when P or MR = LMC. Accounting profit equals average revenue (AR) minus long-run average costs (LAC) and is maximized at Q*.

As previously indicated, an improvement in technology or a decrease in factor prices will shift LAC downward. Since they are mathematically related, a downward shift in LAC (TC/Q) will also shift LMC (ΔTC/ΔQ) to the right. This will increase the profit maximizing rate of production (Q*) and accounting profits. In the long-run, any increase in accounting profits above the average return to capital will tend to cause additional firms to enter the industry. Since accounting profits are a payment to a resource, accounting profits are considered to be a cost in economics. Accounting profits above the average (that is, above average returns to capital) are defined as economic profits. The entry of new firms into the industry in response to economic profits will tend to put downward pressure on output prices and upward pressure on factor prices. This will reduce economic profits. Once accounting profits in an industry or market become equal to the average return to capital new firms will cease entering the market or industry and there will be a long-run equilibrium in which economic profits will tend to be zero.[2]

The only exceptions to the tendency for zero economic profits in the long-run are those industries in which additional firms are blocked from entering and competing. Often the main barrier to entry into an industry consists of government regulations. For example, the government protects the mail delivery service of the U.S. Postal System against competition and, until recently, local cable television and utility companies enjoyed a government protected monopoly status. Lack of competition in protected industries may reduce the incentives to produce efficiently and can create the opportunity for economic profits to exist into the long-run. The protected monopoly status of many police units suggests that production inefficiency may be an explanatory factor to falling homicide clearance rates.

STATISTICAL PROBABILITIES

The probability of an event A, denoted as P(A), can be defined as

$$P(A) \; = \; a/(a + b) = \; \underline{\text{Number of outcomes favorable to A}} . \qquad (2.6)$$
$$\text{Total number of possible outcomes}$$

In (2.6), the letter "a" is the number of possible outcomes favorable to the occurrence of event A and the letter "b" is the number of outcomes that are not favorable to the occurrence of event A. Definition (2.6) assumes that all outcomes are **equally likely** and **mutually exclusive**. **Mutually exclusive** means that if one outcome occurs, the other outcomes cannot. The event whose probability is sought may consist of one or more possible outcomes. For example, if an event A is $A = 2,3,5$ when rolling a die then $a = 3$, $b = 3$ and the probability of event A is $P(A) = 3/6 = 1/2$. In another example, if a fair coin with two faces is tossed up into the air, the probability that it will land with the head facing up is $P(Head) = 1/(1 + 1) = 1/2$.

An **elementary event** is a single possible outcome and cannot be further divided into other events. The collection or totality of possible outcomes is a **sample space**. The **complement** of an event A in the sample space S is the collection of elements that are not in A.

For any two events A_1 or A_2 in sample space S, the probability that either event A_1 or event A_2 occurs -- or that they both occur is written as

$$P(A_1 \text{ or } A_2) - P(A_1) + P(A_2) - P(A_1 \text{ and } A_2). \tag{2.7}$$

If events A_1 and A_2 are **mutually exclusive**, then $P(A_1 \text{ and } A_2) = 0$ and $P(A_1 \text{ or } A_2) = P(A_1) + P(A_2)$. In the case where a die is rolled, for example, the probability that either a 4 or a 5 will occur is $P(4 \text{ or } 5) = 1/6 + 1/6 = 1/3$.

Conditional probabilities are when we are interested in the probability of the occurrence of an event given that another related event has occurred. A conditional probability is denoted, for example, as $P(B_1 | A_1)$ and is read "the probability of B_1 given A_1." If events A_1 and B_1 are any two events in sample space S, the conditional probability of B_1 given A_1 is

$$P(B_1 | A_1) = P(A_1 \text{ and } B_1)/P(A_1) \tag{2.8}$$

where $P(A_1) > 0$.

Joint probabilities are used when we are interested in the probability of the joint occurrence of two or more events. For any two events A_1 and B_1 in sample space S, the joint probability that both A_1 and B_1 occur can be written in either of two ways

$$P(A_1 \text{ and } B_1) = P(A_1)P(B_1 | A_1) = P(B_1)P(A_1 | B_1). \tag{2.9}$$

When two events, say A_1 and B_1, are **statistically independent** conditional and joint probabilities are easier to compute. Two events are **statistically independent** if knowing that one of them has occurred does not effect the probability that the other will occur. For example, in the case where A_1 and B_1 are considered to be statistically independent (such as event A_1 is a Head on the first toss of a fair coin and B_1 is a Head on the second toss of a fair coin) then

$$P(B_1 | A_1) = P(B_1) = 1/2$$
$$P(A_1 | B_1) = P(A_1) = 1/2$$
so that,
$$P(A_1 \text{ and } B_1) = P(A_1)P(B_1) = 1/4.$$

When **sampling is done with replacement** (that is, replacing each item in a population) the basic probabilities of selection remain unchanged. Thus sampling with replacement results in independent events. Samples from large populations are often assumed to leave basic probabilities relatively unchanged so that we may consider events to also be independent.

The **expected value** of a discrete random variable X that takes on the value x with probability $P(x)$ is denoted as

$$E(X) = \sum xP(x) = x_1 P(x_1) + x_2 P(x_2) + \ldots + x_n P(x_n) = \mu \tag{2.10}$$

The expected value $E(X) = \mu$ is a measure of central tendency for probability distributions and the symbol μ stands for the mean of such a distribution. For example, the expected value of rolling a die would be calculated as

$$E(X) = \mu = \sum xP(x) = 1(1/6) + 2(1/6) + 3(1/6) + 4(1/6) + 5(1/6) + 6(1/6)$$
$$= 1/6 + 2/6 + 3/6 + 4/6 + 5/6 + 6/6$$
$$= 2 \, 1/6$$
$$= 3 \, 1/2.$$

58

SUGGESTED READINGS

1.   Walters, A. A. "Production and Cost Functions: An Econometric Survey," *Econometrica* 31 (January-April, 1963): 1- 66.

2.   Gylys, J. "Application of a Production Function to Police Patrol Activity," *The Police Chief* July (1974): 70-72.

CHAPTER 3
CHOICE THEORY AND CRIMINAL BEHAVIOR

This chapter illustrates the fundamental tools of individual choice theory by applying them to the common crime of speeding. Also discussed are the issues related to the optimal level of resources to be allocated towards criminal justice system production. The optimal level of resources involves allocation decisions on the part of individual producing units of the criminal justice system as well as by society as a whole. In this chapter, output is limited to the production of crime deterrence.

The major non-economic theories of crime and criminal behavior are also considered. With respect to the crime of speeding, non-economic theories are found to provide little additional explanatory power.

CONSUMER CHOICE THEORY AND CRIME

The broadly applicable objective of utility maximization implies that consumers attempt to gain the greatest satisfaction from their scarce budget resources by making rational consumer choices. As indicated previously, consumer choices represent only a subset of all possible utility gaining actions. Depending on individual preferences, utility or satisfaction may also be gained from some types of criminal actions or choices. By assuming that the utility maximizing objective also applies to individual criminal choice, it seems reasonable to expect that the theory of consumer choice can be used to explain and predict those criminal actions that appear to based primarily on rational behavior.

Illegal Speeding as an Optimal Choice

The following example will illustrate the ability of the model of consumer choice to predict and explain the decision to commit a crime. Assume, for example, that you are a college student who is driving to class in order to take your final exam. Unfortunately, you fell asleep while studying for the exam and are now very late. You also know that it is your university's policy to not schedule make-up exams for missed finals. While driving to the university you observe that you are now significantly exceeding the legal speed limit.

Can illegal behavior such as speeding be explained in terms of the consumer choice model? The answer is clearly yes. It is really very simple. First, your objective must be defined. This is easy. You are very much aware that you need to minimize the degree to which you are late. Moreover, you realize that if you succeed in achieving this goal you will be much better-off. In economic terminology, being better-off is the same as a gain in utility. Therefore, the objective of maximizing utility (that is, gaining as much utility as possible) requires arriving in class ASAP. Assuming that you are a rational college student, you should consider all actions in which the gains in utility appear to exceed their costs. In this case, it appears that your alternative actions are limited only to those that involve the exact rate of speed that you drive.

In order to correctly predict your behavior in this example it is very important that your attitude toward taking risks is known. Attitudes toward risk can be categorized as risk-seeking, risk-neutral, and risk-avoiding. In this example it is assumed that, like most individuals, you prefer to avoid risky actions. More specifically, it is assumed that you would prefer to avoid the risk of speeding as a means of gaining utility. Since you prefer to avoid risky choices such as incremental mph of illegal speeding it follows that each additional mile per hour of speed in excess of the legal limit will gain you less and less utility at the margin.. In other words, illegal speeding exhibits diminishing marginal utility if you are one who prefers to avoid risk. Diminishing marginal utility for illegal speeding is illustrated by the downward sloping demand curves for illegal speeding in figure 3.1.

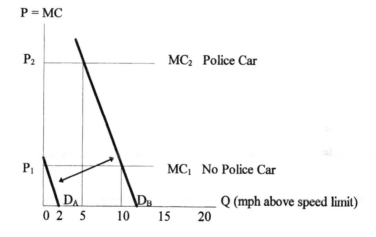

Fig. 3.1. Consumer Demand and Illegal Speeding. Demand curve D_A is relevant when you are not late and demand curve D_B is relevant when you are late. D = MB or MU at any quantity (Q) of excessive speed for demand curves D_A and D_B. Your objective of arriving in class as soon as possible when already late results in an increase in the demand for excessive speed from D_A to D_B. Sighting a police car reduces your optimal choice from 10 mph above the legal speed limit to 5 mph above the legal speed limit and reduces total gains in utility.

In figure 3.1, demand curve D_A represents the marginal utility or benefit gained from illegal speeding when you are not late for class. From 0 to 2 mph of speed above the legal limit, demand curve D_A indicates that the marginal benefit of each mph gains you positive yet diminishing marginal utility. Beginning at 2 mph and beyond, the marginal benefit of each incremental mph of illegal speed on demand curve D_A becomes negative.

Demand curve D_B is the relevant demand curve when you are late for class Demand curve D_B indicates an increased demand for illegal speeding that results from being late for class and is shifted horizontally to the right of demand curve D_A. Demand curve D_B also indicates that each mph of illegal speed in excess of the legal speed limit has a much greater level of marginal utility or benefit.

Assume that you are an experienced driver and have been late for class before. Greater experience and, hence, a greater level of information about consequences, suggests that the demand curves in figure 3.1 will at least approximate optimal choices for illegal speeding. In other words, you know with a relatively high degree of certainty what the benefits of each mph of excessive speed are under each of the two circumstances of late and not late. If there is no police car in sight you also know from experience that there is a relatively low but greater than zero chance of getting a speeding ticket. Assuming that the chance of receiving a speeding ticket is the same for all mph of excessive speed above the legal limit, the marginal cost of each mph of excessive speed is depicted in figure 3.1 as $P_1 = MC_1$.[1] As with the demand or marginal benefit curves, marginal costs are also assumed to be known with a high degree of certainty. Thus when you are late for class (demand curve D_B) and there is no police car in sight the indicated optimal choice is to exceed the legal speed limit by 10 mph.

Now assume that you suddenly see a police car parked by the side of the road. You also note that there is a police officer inside the police car and that there is a radar gun aimed in your direction. Yikes!! On go the brakes. Figure 3.1 indicates that sighting the police car increases the marginal cost of each mph of excessive speed to $P_2 = MC_2$. With the police car sighted, exactly 5 mph above the legal speed limit now produces a marginal benefit of illegal speeding that just equals the now higher marginal cost. The police car makes it irrational for you to exceed the speed limit by more than 5 mph since the marginal benefits along D_B would be less than the marginal costs.

Irrationality translates into consequences that make you worse-off or that would move you away from you goal. For example, you could get a ticket and be much later for class than if you simply reduced your excessive speeding somewhat.

The speeding example illustrates the deterrence hypothesis of crime prevention. The deterrence hypothesis states that less crime will be committed, all else held constant, if there is an increase in the costs and/or a decrease in the benefits of the criminal choice. According to figure 3.1, an increase in the perceived cost of the crime of illegal speeding from $P_1 = MC_1$ to $P_2 = MC_2$ has reduced your optimal choice of excessive illegal speeding by 5 mph. In other words, the total amount of crime (mph of illegal speed) that you would otherwise have committed is now less. Since you have moved back up demand curve D_B the total amount of utility gained from illegal speeding will also be less. In other words, you will arrive later for class than if there was no police car sighted. Notice also that not all criminal behavior is deterred by the police car. Assuming that $P_2 = MC_2$ is an accurate representation of the perceived cost when the police car is sighted it is still optimal for you to choose to exceed the legal speed limit by 5 mph.

Although figure 3.1 illustrates an application of consumer choice theory to the decision to commit the crime of speeding, the theory of consumer choice can be easily applied to many other criminal choices. All that is required is that that the offender have an objective for which crime is an alternative. Moreover, if the offender (that is, someone who has chosen the criminal alternative) appears to be making an attempt to achieve an objective then it can be inferred that the offender is aware of the alternatives and consequences relevant to that objective and is acting as if he or she were rational. If the offender is experienced, or if the consequences of criminal choices are relatively severe, it is also reasonable to assume (unless, of course, the offender has some type of information processing limitation) that the offender has perfect, or near perfect, information about alternatives and consequences.

Later in this chapter the other competing theories of criminal behavior will be discussed in the context of the speeding example. The argument made is that all other non-economic crime theories tend to be more narrowly focused. Consequently, the non-economic crime theories have a more limited range of applicability. On the other hand, economic analysis is much more broadly applicable. In fact, there appears to be no existing theory of crime other than an economic one that can adequately explain and predict the crime of murder as a business decision. The only exceptions to the ability of economics to explain and predict criminal behavior appears to be those crimes in which the basic behavioral assumption of rationality can be genuinely questioned.

Constrained Choice and Deterrence

In the speeding example a hypothetical college student was deterred from 5 mph of illegal speeding because the student sighted a police car. In more general terms, crime deterrence involves many different real factors (including police cars) that provide a disincentive for individuals to choose to commit crimes.

Disincentives to crime can be either positive or negative. Those factors that cause an increase in the costs and/or a decrease in the benefits of crime fall into the category of negative incentives. In the speeding example sighting the police car had a negative incentive effect because the costs of speeding increased. Negative deterrence related factors that increase the costs of crime are among those that are under the control of the criminal justice system. Consequently, criminal justice system deterrence factors can be integrated into the theory of individual choice as costs. Cost factors under the control of the criminal justice system include the level of risk associated with the probability of apprehension, conviction, and punishment as well as the severity of punishment. Like price in the consumer model, an increase in any of the risk related factors or in the level of punishment, all else held constant, is expected to deter criminal choices at the margin.

Cost factors that are not under the control of the criminal justice system include private security personnel and devices such as cameras. Implementing factors such as these are often referred to as "target hardening" by non-economists.

Negative deterrence that results from decreasing the benefits to crime is also possible. An example would be a store policy that involves periodically removing cash from cash registers and placing it in a safe that cannot be opened by employees. Placing a notice that such a policy is being implemented ensures that potential criminal offenders are perfectly informed.

Positive incentives, on the other hand, result from those factors that increase the rewards to legitimate choices relative to crime. Positive incentives, in other words, increase the opportunity cost of criminal alternatives. The existence of an opportunity cost requires two things. One is that the decision maker has at least two alternatives (for example, a criminal choice and a legitimate choice) that achieve the same wants (such as increased wealth). The other is that the decision maker's resources are constrained such that only one alternative can be chosen during a particular period of time. This also means that only one choice can be given up at a time. Thus, even if there are more than two alternatives to consider, the opportunity cost is always the value of the next best choice.

Positive incentives that deter crime include factors such as legitimate job market opportunities and family and community values. Since many objectives that can be achieved through criminal choices (such as greater wealth) may also be achieved through legitimate choices, the greater the value of the choices in the legitimate job market the greater is the opportunity cost of choosing to commit wealth enhancing crimes. At the margin, some wealth enhancing crimes may be deterred through positive incentive effects when the optimal choice appears to be the legitimate one.

Family and community values may also deter crimes through positive incentive effects. Greater rewards for good behavior simply increase the opportunity cost of criminal behavior. For example, communities with higher rates of church membership may tend to have lower crime rates.[2]

The constrained utility-maximization model can be used to illustrate additional negative deterrence or cost factors in the context of the speeding example. The constrained-utility maximization model has two axes--one for each of the two goods that the consumer can choose. Thus there must be two goods for the speeder to choose. Assuming that less of a "bad" (something not wanted) equals a "good" (something wanted), two goods may be created by simply taking the inverses of two bads. Two bads, for example, can be two of the cost or deterrence factors controlled by the criminal justice system. Accordingly, the variable (p) can represent the probability or risk of receiving a speeding ticket and the variable (f) can represent a monetary fine or punishment for speeding. Clearly, (p) and (f) are not wanted and are "bads." They. Assuming that the risk of getting a speeding ticket is greater than zero, the inverse of the "bad" risk (p) is (1/p) and represents a "good" in that as (p) decreases, (1/p) increases. Similarly, decreases in the "bad" punishment (f) will increase (1/f) where (1/f) is defined to be the amount of the other "good" available to the consumer.

As in figure 3.1, decreases in risk (p) reduce the cost of speeding and increase the offender's total utility. In the constrained utility-maximization model decreases in risk (p) increase the amount of good (1/p) and the level of total utility to the consumer.

Figure 3.2 shows the speeding example in terms of the constrained utility-maximization model in which the two goods are (1/p) and (1/f). It is important to note that including the two negative deterrence factors (p and f) in the model implies that all other influential factors, including the probability of conviction, is being held constant.

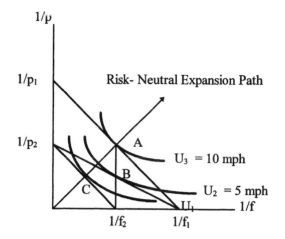

Fig. 3.2. Constrained Utility-Maximization for Speeding. An increase in the probability of apprehension for speeding (such as when a police car is sighted) rotates the budget constraint and decreases the intercept from $1/p_1$ to $1/p_2$. This decreases the total utility of speeding from U_3 to U_2. This translates into arriving later to class than would be the case if the police care were not sighted. If the level of punishment (f) is increased by the same amount as apprehension risk, the budget line shifts inward to $(1/p_2, 1/f_2)$ and the level of utility is maximized at point C on U_1. The risk-neutral indifference curve expansion path indicates that speeders are equally sensitive to changes in (p) and (f).

In figure 3.2, an increase in the probability of apprehension from p_1 to p_2 results from sighting a police car and causes the optimal choice of speeding to be reduced from point A on indifference curve U_3 at 10 mph to point B on indifference curve U_2 at 5 mph.. This is the same result as in figure 3.1 in which there is an increase in $P_1 = MC_1$ to $P_2 = MC_2$ and some marginal benefits along demand curve D_B can no longer be gained. The decrease in utility in figure 3.2 is due to the increase in risk (p) that reduces the availability of good (1/p) as indicated be the change in the intercept on the (1/p) axis. Letting P = price so that the price of good (1/p) is $P_{(1/p)}$ and the price of good (1/f) is $P_{(1/f)}$, the budget constraint slope, given by - $(P_{(1/f)} / P_{(1/p)})(1/f)$, becomes less steep because the "price" of good (1/p) increased relative to the price of good (1/f).

Figure 3.2 also makes it clear that increases in either risk (p) or fines (f) will reduce the level of total utility gained by the speeding college student. To be consistent with the perfect information assumption, an increase in fines (f) could occur, for example, if signs were posted along the road indicating an increase in the level of fines for speeding. If there is an equal percentage increase in the probability of apprehension (p) and the level of fines (f), the budget constraint will shift horizontally inward. An inward horizontal shift is indicated by the parallel budget constraints at $(1/p_2, 1/f_2)$ and a decrease in total utility all the way to point C on indifference curve U_1.

Figure 3.2 assumes risk-neutral preferences for speeding. However, the path of optimal choices associated with equal percentage changes in risk (p) and fines (f) and parallel shifts in the budget constraints may indicate greater responsiveness along either the (1/p) or (1/f) axis depending on a speeder's preferences for risky driving. This is because preferences for more or less risk will be reflected by indifference curves that shift relatively more along either the (1/f) or the (1/p) axis. Regardless of the parallel shifts in the budget constraints, this will cause the points of tangency (optimal choices) to move similarly.

In figure 3.1, the demand curve for illegal speeding is downward sloping and the diminishing marginal utility of each successive mph of illegal speed reflects an offender that prefers to avoid risky driving.[3] It will be shown more clearly in subsequent chapters that risk-averse decision makers tend to be relatively more responsive to changes in the level of punishment (f) than in the probability of apprehension (p). In response to equal percentage changes in (p) or (f) the indifference curves for risk-averse speeders will reflect a preference for good (1/f) by shifting relatively more along the (1/f) axis. In other words, for risk-averse drivers, the changes in optimal choices that occur in response to equal percentage changes in (p) and (f) will reflect relatively greater percentage changes in the consumption of good (1/f).

PRODUCER CHOICE AND DETERRENCE

Considering criminal justice system resources a 1-input aggregate, the two outputs of risk (p) and fines or punishment (f), all else held constant, can produce a level of deterrence for speeding. Making the highly simplified assumption that speeding is the only crime that needs to be deterred the total cost curve for the criminal justice system is illustrated in figure 3.3. The outwardly bowed (or concave to the origin) total cost curve also represents a production possibility frontier (PPF) that shows the maximum level of deterrence attainable with different combinations of (p) and (f) produced. Efficient deterrence production with a given level of resources occurs on the surface of the total cost curve or PPF. The bowed shape of the total cost curve or PPF reflects increasing opportunity costs from shifting resources toward increased production of one output (for example, p) and away from the production of the other output (for example, f). Increasing opportunity costs in production are relatively high (and the total cost curve or PPF is bowed) because resources are specialized in the production of either (p) or (f). If, for example, resources are re-allocated towards (p) and away from (f), those resources less specialized in producing (f) are likely to be re-allocated first. If re-allocation continues, those resources that are more specialized in the production of (f), such as judges and court clerks, will eventually become re-allocated to the production of apprehension risk (p). This will cause more and more units of punishment (f) to be given up for each incremental increase in the production of risk (p). The reallocation of resources runs into diminishing returns and higher opportunity costs in the short-run because resources cannot be retrained in that period of time.

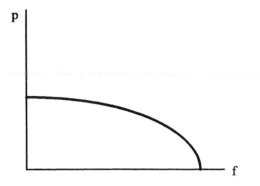

Fig. 3.3. Short-Run Production of (p) and (f). Apprehension risk (p) and fines (f) are two outputs that are produced by the aggregate of criminal justice system resources while holding the probability of conviction constant. The total cost curve or PPF for combinations of (p) and (f) produced is more bowed in the short-run due to specialization. A given amount of criminal justice system resources can produce relatively more of output (f).

In the long-run, diminishing returns and the effects of specialization are less and the production possibility (or total cost) curve is less bowed or concave. Diminishing returns are less because all resources are variable and the longer period of time involved allows for specialized resources to be retrained.

As with straight line cost curves, no combination of outputs (p and f) that lie outside the bowed production possibility frontier is attainable with the available level of criminal justice system resources. Also, any point inside the total cost curve or PPF is not efficient because a higher level of deterrence (i.e., more p and/or f) can be obtained with the amount of resources available.

The production possibility frontier in figure 3.3 is not symmetrical and indicates that more punishment (f) can be produced than risk (p) for a given amount of criminal justice system resources. This appears reasonable because punishment (f) is assumed to consist of only a monetary fine. On the other hand, the production of apprehension risk for speeding (p) should be expected to absorb criminal justice system resources much more quickly.

Figure 3.4 indicates that increasing levels of criminal justice system resources (represented by the outward shifting total cost curve or PPF) can produce increasing levels of deterrence (more of p and/or f) as indicated by the production isoquants Qd_1 and Qd_2. Because deterrence production is a good, the level of deterrence (Qd) is shown to equal a given level of social utility (U). From societies point of view, an optimal and efficient combination of outputs (p) and (f) (or, equivalently, an optimal and efficient allocation of criminal justice system resources) is obtained at the point of tangency between a given total cost curve or PPF and the highest production isoquant (Qd) or level of social utility (U) attainable.

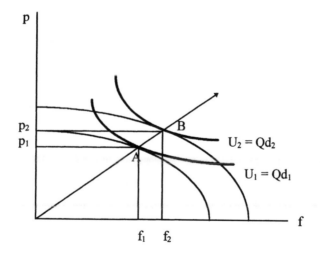

Fig. 3.4. The Production of Apprehension Risk (p) and the Level of Punishment (f). The 2-output and 1-input production model indicates that increasing levels of criminal justice system resources can produce increasing levels of p and f (that is, deterrence) by the outwardly shifting total cost curve or PPF. The points of tangency between a total cost curve and an isoquant (Qd) or social utility curve (U) represents optimal and efficient allocations of criminal justice system resources towards deterrence production.

Isoquants or social utility curves such as (Qd) and (U) in figure 3.4, correspond to a level of deterrence that can be produced with different output combinations of apprehension risk (p) and fines or punishment (f), all else held constant. Social utility has been equated with deterrence output for two reasons. One reason is that deterrence is a good and the other reason is that social utility curves represent preferences. The rate of technical substitution (RTS) between (p) and (f) along a production isoquant such (Qd) and the corresponding of social utility curve (U) should not be the same if driver's (or speeder's) attitudes toward risk can be disaggregated. It is probably true that most drivers tend to be risk-averse. However, if drivers can be disaggregated into two groups such as those with risk-neutral driving preferences and those with risk-averse driving preferences, then a given level of deterrence production will reflect preferences for different combinations of outputs (p) and (f). The preferences for risk-neutral drivers, for example, would be represented by an isoquant (Qd) or social utility curve (U) where (p) and (f) can be substituted for each other rather evenly (an even trade-off would be at a slope of -1) at the point of tangency with the production possibility frontier. This is because risk-neutral drivers are expected to be influenced (that is, deterred) equally by changes in either apprehension risk (p) or punishment (f). In figure 3.5 the production isoquant for risk-neutral drivers is depicted as $U_1 = Qd_1$. For risk-neutral speeders figure 3.5 indicates that the optimal and efficient allocation of resources is one that produces fines or punishment (f_1) and apprehension risk (p_1).

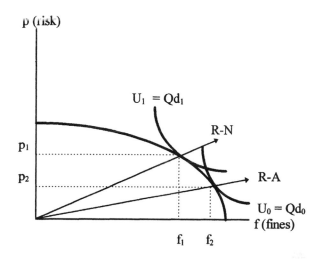

Fig. 3.5. Risk-Neutral and Risk-Averse Drivers. Risk-neutral drivers (R-N) are reflected by social utility curve U_1 and isoquant Qd_1 while risk-averse drivers (R-A) are reflected by social utility curve U_0 and isoquant Qd_0. As drivers (or speeders) are more risk-averse increases in the production of fines or punishment (f) and decreases in the production of apprehension risk (p) reflects the optimal output combination and corresponding allocation of productive resources.

For drivers (or speeders) that are averse to risky driving the social utility curves (U) and corresponding deterrence production isoquants (Qd) must rotate clockwise to become steeper at the point of tangency. This is because the assumed increased sensitivity to changes in punishment (f) relative to changes in apprehension risk (p) by risk-averse speeders suggests that less important risk (p) must be technically substituted for more important punishment (f) at a higher rate (or, at a slope greater than -1) in order to hold the level of deterrence constant. The higher rate of technical substitution (RTS) of (p) for (f) is reflected by social utility curve U_0 and isoquant Qd_0 in figure 3.5. The social utility curves and corresponding production isoquants will also have expansion paths that reflect different preferences for risk.

Although the above analysis is theoretically appealing it may still be too abstract or narrowly focused to be an accurate predictor of deterrence production by units of the criminal justice system. There are at least five additional factors that should be considered.

In the real world there are multiple crimes to be deterred. Thus one factor not considered is that police production may not be separable with respect to different crime categories.[4] In other words, the production of deterrence for speeders may not be separable from the production of deterrence for property crimes, or for that matter, a completely different output such as the solution of other crimes. On the other hand, production may be more separable in larger police units in which there is more specialization among resources. Regardless of different sized police units, when all crimes are considered in the aggregate the optimal and efficient allocation of resources associated with the production of apprehension risk (p) and punishment (f) by the individual units of the criminal justice system may be different from that suggested by figure 3.5.

A second factor not considered is that there may be legal limits on the methods that police units can use to produce apprehension risk (p) and there may be restrictions on the level of punishment or fines (f) that may be imposed by courts. Such limits may, in some cases, cause deterrence production to be inefficient or less than optimal. In other words, production may occur inside the total cost curve or PPF.

A third factor is related to the fact that economic studies show that the production of general crime deterrence reduces crime rates. Because of competition for scarce resources and social preferences that may be based on misinformation, reduced crime rates, in turn, tend to lead to fewer police resources.[5] Because of social allocative preferences some police units may, in effect, be deterred from producing efficient levels of deterrence if their primary goal is to increase police resources.

Fourth, police training may not emphasis the economic rationale behind the production of deterrence to a significant degree. In fact, some criminologists (who may also be involved in police training) may even argue against the deterrence hypothesis. It appears to be likely, therefore, that some criminal justice system personnel may have a negative attitude towards deterrence production. Negative attitudes may be an additional factor that limits the level of social utility or deterrence actually achieved or, equivalently, causes production to be at an inefficient level for some deterrence producing units.

Fifth, some police units may attempt to increase revenue through speed traps. Together, the objective of maximizing revenue and the method of doing so through speed traps is likely to result in an allocation of resources towards the production of risk (p) and fines (f) that is not socially optimal.

The economics of speed traps can be explained by referring to consumers and producers. For consumers that are highly responsive to small price decreases, an increase in total producer revenue can be obtained from a price decrease. For these consumers, this is because the percentage increase in the quantity of sales is greater than the percentage decrease in the price. A similar, but more complicated, rationale holds for the speed trap. Holding the probability of conviction constant, the quantity of apprehended speeders or "actual sales" in a speed trap is inversely related to the level of fines (f) and directly related to the level of apprehension risk (p). In the common case of risk averse speeders who's choice of mph of excessive speed is relatively more sensitive to decreases in fines (i.e., "price"), a greater quantity of induced speeding (i.e., "potential sales") can be obtained by lowering the level of fines (f). If the percentage increase in "actual sales" (apprehended speeders) is greater than the percentage decrease in "price" then total revenue gained from the speed trap will increase. Unfortunately, even assuming that speeders are risk-averse does not assure that lowering fines (f) will result in an increase in total revenue. Consequently, this method of revenue enhancement is less likely to be observed. Instead of decreasing fines (f) the greatest increase in apprehended speeders or "actual sales" from a speed trap will always result from an increase in apprehension risk (p). Thus fines (f), which are the same as "price" or "marginal revenue" can be held constant and an increase in risk (p) will cause the quantity of "actual sales" to increase along with total revenue. Of course, increasing risk (p) should be expected to have an offsetting negative effect on "actual sales" because, even if speeders are risk-averse, some speeding will be deterred and the total set of all speeders from which "actual sales" is obtained will be smaller. For assumed risk-averse speeders, the offsetting deterrence effect of increasing risk (p) may be offset by decreasing "price" or fines (f). Of course, this would only be expected to occur of the percentage decrease in (f) increased the total set of speeders, and hence "actual sales," by at least as great a percentage.

For police units that attempt to maximize revenue through speed traps, the tendency to possibly decrease fines (f) and always increase risk (p) would not be consistent with the optimal production allocation suggested by figure 3.5. This is especially true for risk-averse drivers in which the optimal production of risk and fines was p_2 and f_2. The fact that citizens tend to complain about speed traps indicates that they are, in fact, risk-averse drivers.

THE OPTIMUM LEVEL OF RESOURCES

The analysis of efficient production by individual units of the criminal justice system answers only part of the resource allocation question. Before individual units of the criminal justice system can produce deterrence (efficiently or not) society must first decide what level of resources to provide. In other words, society determines the location of the total cost curve or production possibility frontier (PPF) for criminal justice system producers. If society desired to completely eliminate speeding, then it may be able to do so if enough resources were provided. For example, the college student in the speeding example was deterred from only 5 mph of the possible 10 mph of excessive speeding when one police car was sighted. Assuming again that speeding is the only crime and that the criminal justice system only produces deterrence against speeding, increasing the level of criminal justice system resources aimed at speeders shifts the production possibility frontier outward such as in figure 3.4. If the criminal justice system is efficient and increases the production of apprehension risk (p) and punishment (f), it causes the college student to choose to drive fewer and fewer mph above the legal speed limit.

Increasing the level of criminal justice system resources to deter speeding requires more police officers, police cars, judges, clerks, and other resources. Moreover, increases in resources to the criminal justice system require less alternative spending by other public sector production units. If taxes are increased to finance increased deterrence production then less income can be spent privately. Thus some alternative spending must be given up to reduce the amount of illegal speeding and an opportunity cost must be incurred. Opportunity costs suggest that the optimum amount of speeding from society's viewpoint is likely to be greater than zero.

The optimum amount of speeding is depicted in figure 3.6 in which, from society's viewpoint, decreasing the total amount of mph of illegal speed yields decreasing marginal benefits. The diminishing marginal benefit (MB) curve in figure 3.6 assumes that the most egregious speeders are apprehended and punished (fined) first. Figure 3.6 also indicates that devoting more and more resources towards the deterrence of speeding results in increasing opportunity costs in the production and consumption of alternative goods and services. Opportunity costs increase because as resources are re-allocated spending on less important items occurs first. The optimal social choice for the amount of resources devoted to deterring speeding is the point at which the marginal benefit (MB) of criminal justice system resources allocated toward deterring speeding just equals the marginal opportunity cost (MC) of those same resources in terms of forgone alternative expenditures.

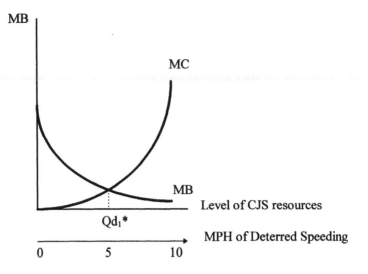

Fig. 3.6. The Optimal Level of Criminal Justice System Resources. The optimal amount of resources devoted to the deterrence of illegal speeding is Qd_1^*. The Qd_1^* level of resources contains one police car at the point at which MB = MC. Any fewer resources than Qd_1^* make society worse off because, at the margin, increasing resources toward deterrence results in social benefits in excess of opportunity costs. Resources in excess of Qd_1^* result in marginal opportunity costs that are greater than marginal deterrence benefits. Since society must give up alternative expenditures in order to produce deterrence, the level of criminal justice system resources at Qd_1^* is not likely to produce levels of risk (p) and fines (f) that are sufficient to deter all mph of illegal speeding.

ALTERNATIVE THEORIES OF CRIMINAL BEHAVIOR

It has been demonstrated that the economic theory of criminal behavior stresses the importance of individual choice in response to changes in opportunities. Opportunities to gain utility (net benefits) are determined by changes in the benefits and costs of relevant alternatives. For example, the speeding college student found that sighting a police car eliminated the opportunity to exceed the speed limit by as much as would otherwise be preferred. Economists would say that the college student behaved as if he or she was rational because the economic model (based on assumed rational behavior) predicted that an increase in perceived costs, all else (including tastes and attitudes toward risk) held constant, would result in less speeding.

A characteristic of the economic theory of individual choice is that it does not distinguish qualitatively between criminal and non-criminal alternatives or choices. All choices and behaviors, criminal and non-criminal, are simply evaluated in terms of their benefits and costs (that is, the opportunities that are presented) within the context of an assumed objective. In contrast, non-economic theories of criminal behavior make qualitative distinctions between criminal and non-criminal choices or behaviors. Non-economic theories also tend to investigate why individuals have particular tastes and preferences that may explain a tendency to make criminal choices. Economic theory simply assumes that tastes and preferences are given during the period of time in which opportunities are acted upon.

Another characteristic of economic choice theory is that it is broadly applicable. On the other hand, because non-economic theories subdivide the overall population in terms of some characteristics (usually these characteristics are related to persons or groups, the environment, or some social process), non-economic theories tend to be less generally applicable in terms of their ability to predict and explain criminal behavior.

The three types of non-economic theories of crime include physiological, psychological, and sociological theories. The most narrowly applicable theories of criminal behavior appear to be the physiological and psychological theories. *Physiological theories* of criminal behavior focus on particular physical characteristics that may predispose a person to commit crimes. Particular physical characteristics include such things as biochemical and chromosome imbalances. Chromosome imbalance theory, for example, is based on the hypothesis that abnormal XYY chromosome males, as opposed to normal XY chromosome males, tend to exhibit relatively more aggressive and asocial behavior. To the extent that this is true it may explain possibly higher incidences of crime among XYY males.

Psychological theories rest on personality disorders to explain criminal behavior. Personality disorders may be due to factors such as events during childhood, improper socialization, and even physiological characteristics. However, psychological theories of crime also suggest that criminal behavior is purposive. For example, persons suffering a guilt complex (or inferiority complex) may commit crimes in order to be punished or, equivalently, to get attention. Because they suggest purposive or goal oriented behavior (that is, that individuals have preferences), psychological theories of criminal behavior are the most consistent with economic theory. Purposive, goal oriented behavior that involves choices suggests that even individuals with personality disorders (for example, guilt and inferiority complexes) are still making rational utility maximizing choices. An economist might even rationalize such behavior by indicating that there is no accounting for taste. A major contribution of psychological theory towards understanding criminal behavior may be that it may help to clarify and explain individual preferences that are often referred to as "psychological motives."

That some individuals commonly though to have personality disorders, such as those who live in the street, may not achieve a very high level of utility does, however, support the inference that some type of mental disorder is influencing their ability to process information. The inability to effectively process information may prohibit such individuals from choosing different objectives and/or generating and evaluating alternatives effectively. This type of "technical inefficiency of the mind" suggests that rational behavior among some individuals is likely to be more bounded.[6]

In many cases it may be difficult to reform or alter physiological and psychological abnormalities that form the basis for unusual tastes and preferences. For example, a child raised in an unstable and violent family environment is likely to always prefer greater excitement and risk. The wide spread dissatisfaction with past and current reform efforts suggests that it may be more pragmatic, as well as more cost effective, to adopt policies aimed at altering the benefits and costs of criminal alternatives rather than attempt to alter or reform tastes and preferences.

Physiological and psychological theories of criminal behavior do not appear to provide a sufficiently general basis for predicting and explaining the behavior of the speeding college student in the above example. If, however, the college student's behavior departs significantly from the average behavior predicted by the model, then perhaps one may suspect that a personality disorder could be the explanatory factor. On the other hand, unpredicted behavior may sometimes be explained by circumstances. A variation in circumstances changes opportunities (that is, benefits and costs). For example, the college student may know that the police officer in the car is their spouse or a close friend or is looking only for drunk drivers. The risk of getting a speeding may be less and the optimal choice of mph may be more if the police officer is a spouse or close friend. If the police officer is known to be looking for drunk drivers the optimal mph may be more if the college student's driving is also non-erratic. In any case, given that crime and criminal behavior is as pervasive as it is, physiological and psychological theories appear to explain only a narrow aspect of it.

Sociological theories of criminal behavior consist mainly of social structure theories and social process theories. In general, *social structure* theories suggest that environmental factors are more responsible for crime than individual choices. *Social process* theories focus on how criminal behavior is learned through different types of social interaction. This could include peer groups, for example.

In some ways sociological theories appear to share some common ground with economic theory. A sociologist may consider that neighborhoods in which guns are easily accessible and that are characterized by crowded living conditions, poor schools, and large numbers of unemployed teenage males are likely to have higher crime rates than neighborhoods without these characteristics. An economist, on the other hand, may consider that variations in circumstances and environmental factors should also be expected to effect opportunities (benefits and costs) for individual utility-maximizing choices. For example, crowded conditions may provide both easier and more frequent opportunities for theft and also increase the chances of maintaining the offender's anonymity. Thus changes in environmental factors that increase costs and/or decrease the benefits of criminal choices appear to be an aspect of social structure.

Another similarity between economic and social process theories is that the level of information that an individual has about alternatives and consequences reflects the learning aspect of many social processes. For example, peers can transfer crime related information gained from experience. In this way social process theory actually supports the assumption of perfect information as it is used in economic models.

Perhaps it is best to think of sociological theories as providing the broader social context within which rational individual choices are made. Psychological and physiological theories appear useful for explaining unusual tastes and preferences. This leaves economic theory to occupy the middle ground and explain most behaviors -- criminal or not.

The relative importance of economic theory in explaining murder as a business decision is particularly important to understand. None of the non-economic theories can be expected to provide an adequate analysis of murder as a business decision. Psychological theories can add only a limited amount of specificity to the relatively narrowly defined wealth related preferences of business-like murderers. Professional criminals are also known to be relatively insensitive to socio-economic factors such as the availability of legitimate wealth producing alternatives. This suggests that the broader social context theories are also less applicable. Thus it appears that the analysis of murder as a business decision is a job that is best suited for economics.

SUGGESTED READINGS

1. Sollars et al., "Drug Enforcement and the Deterrence of Property Crime Among Local Jurisdictions," *Public Finance Quarterly* (January 1994): 22-45.

2. Hull, B. B. and F. Bold, "Preaching Matters: Replication and Extension." *Journal of Economic Behavior and Organization* 27 (June 1995):143-149.

3. Darrough and Heineke, *The Multi-Output Translog Production-Cost Function: The Case of Law Enforcement Agencies.* In *ECONOMIC MODELS OF CRIMINAL BEHAVIOR,* ed. J. M. Heineke. Amsterdam: North Holland, 1978, 259-302.

4. Cloninger, D. O. "Enforcement Risk and Deterrence: A Re-examination," *Journal of Socio-Economics* 3 (Fall 1994): 273-85.

5. Tauchen, H. et al., "Criminal Deterrence: Revisiting the Issue With a Birth Cohort," *Review of Economics and Statistics* 76 (August 1994): 399-412.

PART II. MURDER AS A BUSINESS DECISION

CHAPTER 4
THEORETICAL ASPECTS OF MURDER AS A BUSINESS DECISION

This chapter illustrates the application of economic analysis to the crime of murder as a business decision. For business-like murder's the appropriate level of information is determined to be decision making under conditions of risk. A subjective expected utility (SEU) model that assumes decision making under conditions of risk is developed and applied in a hypothetical example. In the context of the SEU model, the explanatory power and predictions of economic theory appear to be very reasonable. The SEU model can also be simplified into a three-equation mathematical form. An important point is that different levels of information appear to be critical when the decision to commit murder is business-like.

THE APPROPRIATE LEVEL OF INFORMATION

In choice theory models such as those for consumers and producers, the level of information available to the decision maker was assumed to be perfect. The decision maker is assumed to be aware of all possible alternatives that may achieve an objective and the consequences of each alternative are assumed to be known. In terms of decision theory, the perfect information assumption means that decisions are made under circumstances of certainty. In other words, there is a probability of 1.0 that particular outcomes or consequences will occur. Since all relevant alternatives and their associated outcomes are known, it is possible to make an optimal choice. In other words, the consumer can maximuze utility and the producer can minimize costs and maximize profit.

Perfect information is often used only as a simplifying assumption in models developed more for pedagogical purposes. Relaxing the assumption of perfect information results in a less abstract or more realistic model in which optimization is less likely. Having less than perfect information for decision making involves conditions of either risk or uncertainty.

When decisions are made under conditions of uncertainty, information levels are insufficient to allow even subjectively determined probabilities to be attached to outcomes. Well-known decision models such as maximax, maximin, and minimax among those that are often used. Decision making under conditions of uncertainty is unlikely to be generally applicable to the analysis of murder as a business decision. This is because an unfavorable outcome or consequence can be severe. When very important decisions are made, such as those with very severe consequences, it is reasonable to expect that most offenders (whether they are motivated on the basis of rational calculation or by powerful emotions) will seek to acquire a greater level of information. Moreover, the greater level of information expected to be available for important decisions suggests that a model that fully exploits this information is appropriate.

With decision making under conditions of risk the decision maker is not certain of the outcome or consequences of a choice. Instead, the decision maker has only enough information to assign subjective probabilities to the outcomes of relevant alternatives. By not requiring that the highest possible level of information be available to the decision maker, conditions of risk are much more realistic and widely applicable. The most appropriate level of information for murder as a business decision appears to be decision making under conditions of risk. In terms of the level of information available to the decision maker, decision making under conditions of risk dominates the middle ground between perfect information and uncertainty. Moreover, perfect information can easily be incorporated into a decision model that assumes conditions of risk by assigning a probability of 1.0 or 0.0 to the outcomes.

THE SEU MODEL OF MURDER AS A BUSINESS DECISION

Relaxing the more restrictive assumption of perfect information and assuming conditions of risk requires a decision model with a higher level of complexity. A well known and widely applied decision model that assumes conditions of risk is the subjective expected utility (SEU) model. In the SEU model it is assumed that the decision maker can subjectively assign probabilities (where the probabilities are assumed to not reflect certainty) to the occurrence of each outcome or state of nature. The consideration of consequences (in terms of subjectively assigned probabilities) means that rational behavior is assumed by the SEU model. The SEU model can also be extended to reflect perfect information or certainty by assuming outcome probabilities of either 1.0 or 0.0. The assumption of rational behavior and the ability to incorporate decision making under conditions of both risk and certainty are two factors that make the SEU model highly useful to the analysis of murder as a business decision.

Usefulness is necessary but insufficient, the SEU model would still not be appropriate for the analysis of murder as a busines decision if the offender's objectives did not include wealth or the offender would not consider murder a relevant alternative. Therefore, it is important to state formally that an offender's objective(s) when committing murder as a business decision are assumed to include wealth. However, even for highly materialistic wealth seekers, murder is still likely to be considered a qualitatively inferior alternative. On the other hand, for wealth seekers who have low morals (or a limited set of values) and who are capable of being callous, at least to the victim, the crime of murder may be perceived as the qualitative equal to any other relevant alternative. Once the offender's wealth objective and callousness is assumed, an economic analysis of murder as a business decision in terms of the SEU model becomes entirely appropriate.

A business-like murder in which the offender prefers or seeks gains in personal wealth is developed in the following hypothetical example. Although this example is strictly hypothetical, it is intended to be relevant to actual cases that are generally similar. Assume, for example, that Mr. and Mrs. X have been married to each other for many years. Unfortunately for Mrs. X, Mr. X has a paramour named Ms. Y with whom he has been spending more and more time. In fact, his relationship with young and single Ms. Y has progressed to the point that Mr. X would prefer to no longer be married to Mrs. X. Instead, Mr. X would now prefer to be married to young Ms. Y. Compounding Mr. X's problems is the fact that during his marriage to Mrs. X a substantial amount of personal property has been accumulated. Mr. and Mrs. X also have several young children. As it happens, Mr. X would prefer to retain the custody of his children and as much of the accumulated property as possible.

Assuming that Mr. X has become sufficiently callous towards Mrs. X he may no longer value the well-being of Mrs. X. The lack of concern for Mrs. X's well being may, in part, be the result of Mr. X falling in love with young Ms. Y and out of love with Mrs. X. At least from Mr. X's point of view, this suggests that Mr. and Mrs. X no longer have interdependent utilities. The lack of interdependent utilities suggests that Mr. X may be more unfeeling and callous towards Mrs. X. Of course, if Mr. and Mrs. X have a particularly acrimonious relationship it may also be that Mr. X would gain additional psychic utility from murdering his spouse. In this case Mr. X's preferences should have a multi-attributed structure rather than only a single-attribute such as wealth. This does not create a problem with the SEU model if (as in this example) it is assumed that monetary equivalents for legal and illegal activities exist.[1] Thus it may be that Mr. X considers three relevant and, from his point of view, qualitatively equal alternatives that may achieve his objectives: Choice 1). Divorce Mrs. X. Choice 2). Murder Mrs. X. Choice 3). Take no action.

If Mr. X remains concerned with Mrs. X's well being and adheres to a normal standard of moral conduct, the murder alternative is unlikely to be considered qualitatively equal to the other relevant alternatives. It is also possible that Mr. X prefers that Mrs. X retain custody of his children and property. This would then make the murder alternative entirely irrelevant.

When decisions are made under conditions of risk, such as with the SEU model, the consequences of each alternative are referred to either as "states of nature" or as "outcomes." States of nature (outcomes) are either favorable or unfavorable to the decision maker. The decision maker is assumed to be able to subjectively determine the probability of occurrence of each state of nature (outcome) for each relevant alternative. In this example, the states of nature (outcomes) for Mr. X's three alternatives are defined as follows. If Mr. X chooses to divorce Mrs. X he may lose either less personal property than expected (the favorable outcome) or he may lose all personal property (the unfavorable outcome). For simplicity, it is assumed that marrying young and single Ms. Y and losing custody of his children to Mrs. X are additional outcomes that occur with the divorce choice and that the values of these two outcomes to Mr. X are exactly offsetting. This reduces the complexity of the divorce choice outcomes such that personal property (i.e., wealth) is the only issue. For the murder alternative, the favorable outcome is that Mr. X is not apprehended (that is, he gets away with it) and the unfavorable outcome is that Mr. X is apprehended, convicted and punished (that is, he does not get away with it). If Mr. X gets away with the murder, it is assumed that he retains custody of his children, marries Ms. Y, and retains possession of all accumulated property. If Mr. X does not get away with the murder he receives punishment and loses all benefits associated with getting away with it. For the take no action alternative, the favorable outcome is the status quo arrangement. In other words, things remain exactly as they are. The unfavorable outcome is that Mrs. X threatens to file for divorce unless Mr. X quits seeing Ms. Y.

For illustrative purposes it is necessary to assume that there is an amount of money that can be associated with any of the different possible outcomes such that Mr. X is indifferent between the money and the outcome. This is easy for outcomes that have a market value such as with personal property. However, it is possible that murdering Mrs. X, marrying Ms. Y, and retaining the custody of his children may result in additional psychic gains. Psychic gains are "utility" in the strict economic sense. If, on the other hand, it is assumed that psychic gains have monetary equivalents then "utility" becomes a cardinal measure of value in the von Neumann and Morgenstern sense. The von Neumann and Morgenstern concept of utility as a measurable value is commonly used as a basis for choice making in situations involving risk. In essence, von Neumann and Morgenstern utility translates the subjective expected utility of each choice into a straight forward expected monetary value. Thus offender preferences in the SEU model are structured as having wealth as the only argument (attribute). In other words, Mr. X's only objective is assumed to be personal wealth enhancement.

Table 4.1 summarizes Mr. X's decision alternatives in terms of expected monetary values (EMV) and corresponding levels of subjective expected utility (SEU). The EMV for the states of nature (outcomes) of each of the three choices have been arbitrarily chosen for the purpose of illustration.

Table 4.1
Decision Table with Probabilities and Expected Monetary Values

Alternatives	$'s Favorable (S₁)	$'s Unfavorable (S₂)	($'s) EMV of SEU
1. Divorce	10,000	-1,000,000	-495,000
2. Murder	5,000,000	-10,000,000	-2,500,000
3. No Action	3,000,000	-2,000,000	500,000
Probabilities	$P(S_1) = 0.5$	$P(S_2) = 0.5$	

If Mr. X has as much information as the average person about the likely consequences of each of the three choices he definitely does not have perfect information. Let us say that in the absence of additional information Mr. X considers that favorable and unfavorable states of nature (outcomes) are equally likely for each choice. In other words, the subjectively determined probability (p) of any outcome is p = 0.5 regardless of which choice is made. Although the following assumptions are obvious, they should be still be stated. It is assumed that the favorable or unfavorable states of nature (outcomes) for each choice are mutually exclusive. Thus if one state of nature (outcome) occurs the other cannot occur. All events are elementary events because they consist of a single possible outcome: favorable or unfavorable. Also, the event probabilities for each choice are, at this point, assumed to represent all possible outcomes in a sample space (S). Thus the sum of the event probabilities for each choice is (1.0).

Assuming that the variable X is a random variable that takes on the monetary values of the favorable and unfavorable outcomes for each choice in Table 4.1, the expected value equation (2.10) can be used to calculate the expected monetary value (EMV) of each choice. Thus we have $E(X) = \Sigma x P(x) = x_1 P(x_1) + x_2 P(x_2) = $ EMV (or SEU) for each choice.

1) Divorce Mrs. X $= [P(S_1) \times \$ \text{ Value of } S_1] + [P(S_2) \times \$ \text{ Value of } S_2]$

$= (0.5 \times \$10,000) + (0.5 \times -\$1,000,000)$

$= \$5,000 - \$500,000$

$= -\$495,000.$

2) Murder Mrs. X $= (0.5 \times \$5,000,000) + (0.5 \times -\$10,000,000)$

$= \$2,500,000 - \$5,000,000$

$= -\$2,500,000.$

3) Take No Action $= (0.5 \times \$3,000,000) + (0.5 \times -\$2,000,000)$

$= \$1,500,000 - \$1,000,000$

$= \$500,000.$

Using the EMV or corresponding level of SEU all three choices can be ranked from best to worst. In order for Mr. X to maximize EMV or SEU Mr. X must choose the alternative with the highest EMV or SEU. In this case Mr. X's best choice is (3): "take no action" where the EMV = SEU = $500.000. In other words, during the period of time in which the alternatives are being considered the expected value of the status quo is $500.000.

According to table 4.1, Mr. X's next best alternative is choice (1): "divorce Mrs. X." This makes divorcing Mrs. X the opportunity cost of optimal choice (3). Note that the expected monetary value (EMV) or level of SEU of Mr. X's opportunity cost is -$495,000. Thus Mr. X is strongly influenced to choose choice (3) and take no action. As it turns out Mr. X is even more strongly influenced to avoid choice (2): "murder Mrs. X" where the EMV = SEU = -$2,500,000.

Given the circumstances as described in this example, the predictions of economic theory are probably fairly consistent with reality. Moreover, there are some additional implications. If, for example, Mr. X makes the optimal status quo choice the unfavorable outcome (in which Mrs. X files for divorce unless Mr. X quits seeing Mrs. Y) may occur. If Mrs. X files for divorce over the issue of Ms.

Y, this would remove choice (1): "divorce Mrs. X" from Mr. X's consideration. Assuming that Mr. X can generate no new alternatives he then has only two remaining alternatives: Choice (3) "Take No Action" or Choice (2) "Murder Mrs. X." Moreover, the take no action alternative would now be assigned the monetary value of -$2,000,000 with certainty. This approaches very close to the EMV or SEU of the murder alternative. This suggests that, as a general rule, there is a greater tendency for homicides to occur when one spouse attempts to divorce the other.

There is also the possibility that additional nonspecified outcomes could occur. In other words, the favorable and unfavorable outcomes of choices (1) and (3) do not actually include all possible events in sample space S. For example, if Mr. X chooses either choice (1) "divorce Mrs. X" or (3) "take no action," Mrs. X could still die by natural causes, be killed in a traffic accident, be hit by lightning, or some other remote possibility. From callous Mr. X's point of view the effect of additional but remotely possible outcomes would be to increase the number of favorable outcomes and lower the probabilities of the unfavorable outcomes. This would increase the EMV or SEU of choices (1) and (3) relative to choice (2), the murder alternative.

THE EFFECT OF PERFECT INFORMATION

Now suppose that Mr. X has an acquaintance named Mr. Z who is a member of a professional criminal organization. As it also turns out, Mr. X is a highly respected lawyer with many powerful political and law-enforcement connections. Because of Mr. X's law-enforcement connections and status in the legal profession, Mr. X also has the potential to become a police commissioner, State's Attorney General, or other influential public official. Mr. Z is instructed by his organization to contact Mr. X and tell him that highly experienced professional hit-men can be made available to Mr. X at no cost. The hit-men are offered for "free" to Mr. X because Mrs. X's murder may be useful to the criminal organization. With a police "insider" like Mr. X under their control, Mr. Z's criminal organization will always know what investigations the police are conducting. This will make the police completely ineffective against Mr. Z's criminal organization. Reducing costs in this way will maximize the criminal organization's profit. This scenario is even more likely if, due to a previous undercover investigation, some members of Mr. Z's criminal organization have been arrested.

Ultimately, the criminal organization is interested in making more money. Moreover, the members of the criminal organization do not care how they get the money. Like Mr. X, they are also callous individuals who would not be concerned about murdering Mrs. X. Thus Mr. Z's criminal organization may be interested in even more than creating a "mole" like Mr. X.[2] By helping Mr. X and the police apprehend small-time criminals who are operating illegally in markets such as gambling, prostitution, and drugs the criminal organization would make Mr. X and the police look good to the general public. It would also create near perfect monopolies in all of these markets for the criminal organization.

In order to enter into these markets and operate successfully, the criminal organization needs to be able to fully exploit Mr. X's political connections. It also needs Mr. X to continue to help protect its members against criminal investigation and/or legal sanctions. Mr. X's full cooperation as a mole, and perhaps as a facilitator to the further expansion of organized criminal enterprise, is guaranteed because of the leverage the criminal organization gains by involving him in the murder of Mrs. X. Mrs. X must be "set up" to be murdered. In other words, if hit-men travel any significant distance they must be certain that on their arrival the victim will be present at the designated place. "Setting up" Mrs. X is a job more easily accomplished by Mr. X and has the effect of directly involving him in the murder.

According to organized crime's Mr. Z, the use of the highly experienced hit-men assures that there is absolutely no chance that Mr. X would ever be connected to or implicated in Mrs. X's murder. The hit-men know how to stage the crime scene so that it will not appear that organized crime is involved or that Mr. X committed the crime himself.[3] They also know how to commit a murder without leaving evidence that would connect either the criminal organization or Mr. X to the crime scene. Also, and very importantly, the criminal organization has the ability to enforce secrecy so that it is very unlikely that information about Mrs. X's murder will be leaked to the police before or after the murder. In effect, the use of professional hit-men and the enforcement of secrecy increase the level of information about the consequences of the murder alternative substantially. Given highly experienced and professional hit-men it is now reasonable to assume that Mr. X now has perfect information with regard to the murder alternative.

Of course, it may also be that the local police department will be intimidated by Mr. X and his political contacts. A "cowardly lion" police department will also play into the hands of Mr. X and his professional criminal colleagues by further reducing the risk of apprehension and conviction.

The probability for the favorable (S_1) murder outcome would now be certain and can be set to $p = 1.0$. Moreover, because the outcomes are mutually exclusive, the probability of the unfavorable (S_2) murder outcome can be set to $p = 0.0$. With decision making under conditions of certainty now assured, Mr. X calculates the EMV or SEU for the murder alternative as:

$$\text{EMV or SEU} = (1.0 \times \text{\$ Value of the best outcome of either } S_1 \text{ or } S_2)$$
$$= (1.0 \times \$5,000,000)$$
$$= \$5,000,000.$$

Given that the expected monetary value (EMV) and the corresponding level of subjective expected utility (SEU) of the two other alternatives--divorce Mrs. X and take not action--can be assumed to remain the same, the best choice for Mr. X is now the murder alternative. In terms of wealth gains, Mrs. X's murder is now expected (with certainty) to be worth \$5,000,000 to Mr. X. Given the values assigned to the outcomes in this example, this is ten times the wealth of the next best "take no action" choice.[4]

If Mr. X now chooses to murder Mrs. X, his opportunity cost is the take no action (status quo) choice in which EMV = SEU = $500,000. The least favorable choice now is to divorce Mrs. X where the EMV = SEU = -$495,000. When hit-men were not available divorcing Mrs. X was the second best choice. Thus it would clearly be a mistake for Mr. X to file for divorce and/or appear to go through the motions of divorcing Mrs. X prior to her murder. Though Mr. X would appear to be acting legitimately, he would also be choosing either the second or least best choice. That would be irrational unless, of course, Mr. X was certain that he would never actually end up in divorce court.

The expected value of the perfect information (PI), or equivalently the expected value of using professional hit-men and entering into a permanent partnership with organized crime, can also be calculated. The value of perfect information (PI) is calculated as the expected monetary value (EMV) of the best choice with perfect information minus the EMV of the best choice without PI. That is,

Value of PI = (EMV of the best choice with perfect information) - (EMV of the best choice without perfect information)

= $5,000,000 - $500,000

= $4,500,000.

In this example, the value of perfect information of $4,500,000 is nearly equal to the value of the best choice with perfect information of $5,000,000. This is because the value of the best choice without perfect information is significantly less. In other words, the value of perfect information to a business-like murderer such as Mr. X is indicated to be quite high.

MURDER CONSEQUENCES AS EVENTS

As indicated, an additional state of nature (outcome) that could result from the "divorce Mrs. X" or the "take no action" alternatives is that, for various reasons not related to Mr. X, Mrs. X could still die. There are also additional elementary outcomes that may result from the murder alternative. It was assumed that if Mr. X "does not get away with it" he is apprehended, convicted, and punished or that if Mr. X "gets away with it" he is simply not apprehended. A more thorough delineation of outcome possibilities for the murder alternative is provided in table 4.2. Note that the occurrences of some events (outcomes) in table 4.2 depend upon the occurrence of other related events. Such events require that conditional probabilities be provided.

Table 4.2
Murder Consequences with Conditional Probabilities

Aggregated Events (Outcomes or States of Nature S) ———————————→	Elementary Events	Conditional Probabilities for Elementary Events
	Execution	$(Pa)(Pc|a)(Pe|c)$
Apprehended (Unfavorable S_2) ⟨ Convicted of Murder ⟨	Imprisonment	$(Pa)(Pc|a)(1-Pe|c)$
Convicted of a Lesser Offense or Acquital ——→	Other Punishment	$(Pa)(1-Pc|a)$
Not Apprehended ——————————————→ (Favorable S_1)	No Punishment	$(1-Pa)$

Source: Based on I. Ehrlich, "The Deterrent Effect of Capital Punishment: A Question of Life and Death," *American Economic Review* 65 (1975) p. 397.
Note: The event probabilities are defined as follows:
Pa = The probability of apprehension.
$1-Pa$ = The probability of not being apprehended and is the complement of Pa.
$Pc|a$ = The conditional probability of a murder conviction given apprehension.
$1-Pc|a$ = The probability of conviction for a lesser offense or acquittal given apprehension and is the complement of $Pc|a$.
$Pe|c$ = The probability of being executed given a murder conviction.
$1-Pe|c$ = The probability of not being executed given a murder conviction and is the complement of $Pe|c$.

The conditional probabilities in table 4.2 make it clear that rationally motivated business-like murderers can only achieve their objective if there is very little chance of apprehension, conviction, or punishment. In fact, it appears that an offender is likely to focus attention on reducing the probability of apprehension (Pa) since the probabilities for both conviction and punishment are conditional. For example, it can be assumed that a significant increase in the level of information (such as with highly experienced professional hit-men) will reduce the probability of apprehension to near zero. Referring to table 4.2, when the probability of apprehension (Pa) = 0.0 the probability of not being apprehended $(1- Pa)$ = 1.0. Moreover, when (Pa) = 0.0 the conditional probabilities for conviction and punishment also equal 0.0. In other words, an offender that reduces the probability of apprehension (Pa) to zero, or very near zero, can make criminal sanctions such as conviction and punishment irrelevant to the decision to commit the crime.

A LESS COMPLEX MODEL

Keeping track of all relevant choices and their possible outcomes makes for a rather complex decision model. In terms of actual decision processes, it is probably more realistic to develop a version of the SEU model that simplifies comparisons among alternatives. Such a model can be developed in terms of the following three equations.[5]

$$EU_{hj} = p_j U_j (G_j - f_j) + (1-p_j)U_j (G_j) \qquad (4.1)$$
$$EU_{lj} = U_j (Y_j) \qquad (4.2)$$
$$H_j = H_j (EU_{hj} - EU_{lj}). \qquad (4.3)$$

Equation (4.1) defines the expected utility of a homicide (EU_h) that an individual offender (j) may gain. In equation (4.1) the variable G_j represents the wealth gains to offender j from choosing to commit homicide (h). The disutility or cost of punishment is represented by the variable (f_j). The variable (p_j) is the probability of being arrested and ($1-p_j$) is the probability of not being arrested. It is assumed that $1 \geq p_j \geq 0$ and that $p_j + (1-p_j) = 1.0$. Also, if (p_j) is greater than zero, then individual offender (j) is assumed to make a decision under conditions of risk. The utility level reached by offender (j) if not arrested is $U_j (G_j)$ while $U_j (G_j - f_j)$ is the utility level if arrested. If $f_j > 0$, then $U_j (G_j) > U_j (G_j - f_j)$. It can also be shown that EU_{hj} is inversely related to (p_j) and (f_j).[6]

Offender (j's) utility function (the utility function is a summary of the aspect of (j's) preferences or wants that pertain to the homicide) is indicated by U_j.

Offender (j's) preferences are assumed to be single attributed so that U_j is a wealth function with only one argument (G).

Assuming that wealth seeking offender (j) is sufficiently callous such that homicide (h) is considered a relevant alternative and that homicide (h) is also the best illegitimate alternative, offender (j) will compare the expected utility of the homicide alternative (EU_h) to the expected utility gained by the best legitimate alternative (EU_l) where

$$EU_{lj} = U_j(Y_j). \qquad (4.2)$$

For the legitimate alternative it is assumed that U_j remains a single attributed wealth function in which (Y) represents wealth gains.

Given equations (4.1) and (4.2), the decision to commit homicide (h) by offender (j) (denoted as homicide H_j) becomes a function of

$$H_j = H_j(EU_{hj} - EU_{lj}). \qquad (4.3)$$

Equation (4.3) says that individual (j) chooses to commit homicide (h) only if EU_{hj} - EU_{lj} > 0. In other words, H_j occurs only if the expected wealth gains (G) from homicide (h) are greater than the expected wealth gains (Y) from the next best legitimate choice. Thus it can be inferred that when a homicide occurs wealth gains (Y) are seen as an opportunity cost by offender (j). The propensity to choose the homicide alternative (H_j) depends directly on the expected utility of (G) and inversely on the criminal justice system variables (p) and (f) and the value of the legitimate opportunity cost (Y).

Equations (4.1), (4.2), and (4.3) comprise a three-equation model that reflects a decision process in which the offender is assumed to be able to rank relevant alternatives (for example, divorce Mrs. X, take no action, or murder Mrs. X) in terms of subjective expected utility (SEU) and then make the best choice.

Because the conditions of risk assumed by the SEU model imply that the von Neumann and Morgenstern concept of utility as a measure of value (e.g., dollars) is being used, the utility functions for the homicide and legitimate alternatives are assigned a monetary value. In other words, wealth (as either G or Y) is the only argument in the utility functions. Consequently, the offender's objective is assumed to be tangible and equivalent to some measurable level of wealth. It is necessary to also assume the marginal benefit of wealth to offender (j) remains nonnegative.

Existing empirical evidence adds strong support to the assumption that wealth is commonly sought by homicide offenders. For example, many cross-sectional studies[7] indicate that measures related to low legitimate monetary opportunity cost (Y) are consistently related to increases in the rate of homicides (H). This suggests that wealth gains (G) is an argument or attribute in the utility function of most homicide offenders.

It is predictable that less educated or competitive individuals will, on the average, gain less wealth from legitimate choices than more educated and more competitive individuals. All else equal, equation (4.3) predicts that more homicides will be committed by less educated and poorer individuals because such individuals are more often likely to expect greater wealth gains from the homicide alternative.

On the other hand, it would be incorrect to say that less educated and poorer individuals tend to commit more homicides because they have nothing to lose. Poorer and less educated homicide offenders usually make some attempt to avoid being apprehended. There would not be any reason to avoid apprehension if there was nothing to lose. Although it may seem surprising, it may often be that poorer and less educated homicide offenders actually have more to lose (in terms of expected value) than those offenders who are more educated and\or wealthier. This is because poorer and less educated offenders may be less calculating and have fewer resources (such as professional hit-men) with which to plan and carryout a murder for profit. Consequently, the risk of apprehension (and the conditional risk of conviction and punishment) may be significantly higher than for a wealthy and educated offender.

It should be pointed out that the focus on assumed wealth gains may limit the applicability of the SEU model to business-like murders in which the enhancement of personal wealth is what is actually sought by the offender or offenders. For example, the preferences (objectives) of serial-killers and political terrorists (including those who commit hate crimes) are considered to be significantly different. There are indications that serial-killers and political terrorists seek mainly psychic gains. Although an ordinal preference ranking should be possible, a utility function characterized by psychic gains cannot not be assigned a measured or cardinal value in the von Neumann Morgenstern sense. Instead, the utility function would represent the offender's own subjective evaluation of the satisfaction derived from the homicide and, thereby, be consistent with utility only in the strict economic sense.

Inexperienced Offender

The three equation model can be used to illustrate the previous example in which Mr. X may be the type of person who would consider the murder of his spouse Mrs. X in an attempt to gain wealth. At first, Mr. X was without professional assistance from Mr. Z's criminal organization and was considering the three alternatives of divorcing, murdering, or taking no action against Mrs. X. This left Mr. X relatively uncertain about the outcomes of each of the three alternatives--especially for the homicide. In order to apply the three-equation mathematical model Mr. X needs to determine the values for the probability of apprehension (p), punishment (f), homicide gains (G), and legitimate gains (Y). The probability of apprehension (p) can be set equal to the probability of the unfavorable outcome of the murder alternative. In the absence of perfect information this would be (p) = 0.5. Thus the probability of not being apprehended would be $(1 - p) = 0.5$. The wealth related gains (G) from the homicide can be set equal to the value of the favorable outcome of the murder alternative so that (G) = \$5,000,000. The disutility of punishment (f) can be set to equal the value of the unfavorable murder outcome so that (f) = -\$10,000,000. Last, the wealth gains from the legitimate choice (Y) can be set equal to the expected monetary value (EMV) of the best legitimate alternative. The best legitimate alternative was the "take no action" (status quo) choice so that Y = \$500,000. Substituting these values into the mathematical model gives:

$$EU_{hj} = p_j U_j (G_j - f_j) + (1-p_j)U_j (G_j)$$
$$= .5(\$5,000,000 - \$10,000,000) + .5(\$5,000,000)$$
$$= \$0.$$

$$EU_{lj} = U_j (Y_j)$$
$$= \$500,000.$$

$$H_j = H_j (EU_{hj} - EU_{lj})$$
$$= \$0 - \$500,000$$
$$= -\$500,000.$$

Since $(EU_{hj} - EU_{lj}) = -\$500,000$, Mr. X expects to be worse-off from the murder alternative and, therefore, does not choose to murder Mrs. X. Instead, Mr. X chooses the legitimate alternative worth \$500,000. This is the same outcome as before.

Experienced Offender

Two scenarios have been developed that emphasize the effect of increased levels of information on Mr. X's decision. In the first scenario Mr. X is assumed to be a poorer, less educated business-like murderer with no political or law enforcment conections. Consequently, Mr. X must use less experienced "hit-men" and is without the benefits of enforceable secrecy provided by a criminal organization. The level of information is increased but decision making is still made with less than perfect information. The second scenario incorporates the same highly experienced "hit-men" and enforceable secrecy as offered before by Mr. Z's criminal organization. In the second scenario Mr. X can choose optimally because the level of information is perfect.

The effect of Better Information

If Mr. X is a poorer and less educated individual with fewer resources at his disposal, Mr. X may still consider carrying out the planned murder of his spouse Mrs. X. It is assumed that Mr. X's hit-men are affordable but not the best available. Organizational specialization would provide Mr. X an alibi so that he could not be directly linked to the crime scene. However, strict secrecy cannot be assured and, therefore, there is the possibility of the police becoming aware of the conspiracy to murder Mrs. X. Mr. X should still be more certain about the consequences and so the level of decision making information should be considered to be higher.

Let us assume that Mr. X figures that the odds against being apprehended are about four to one. Since only one out of five possible outcomes leads to arrest this subjectively determines that the probability of apprehension as (p) = 0.2. Assuming that the values of (G) and (Y) remain the same as before, applying the three equation model gives

$$
\begin{aligned}
EU_{hj} &= p_j U_j (G_j - f_j) + (1-p_j) U_j (G_j) \\
&= 0.2(\$5,000,000 - \$10,000,000) + 0.8(\$5,000,000) \\
&= -\$1,000,000 + \$4,000,000 \\
&= \$3,000,000
\end{aligned}
$$

$$EU_{lj} = U_j(Y_j) = \$500,000$$

$$H_i = H_i(EU_{hi} - EU_{li})$$
$$= \$3,000,000 - \$500,000$$
$$= \$2,500,000$$

By decreasing the risk of apprehension to $p = 0.2$, the homicide choice (H_j) is expected to be worth \$2,500,000 to Mr. X. Thus homicide (H_j) would be among the set of rational alternatives available for consideration. Although Mr. X is still making decisions under conditions of risk, the increase in the level of information and efficiency gained by employing the hit-men and specializing appears to be worth a great deal (\$2,500,000 - \$500,000 = \$2,000,000) in terms of expected wealth gains.

The "take no action" alternative in which the gains in (Y) are expected to be \$500,000 is Mr. X's next best legitimate alternative. However, if Mr. X is unwilling to remain married to Mrs. X and will only consider divorce to be his next best legitimate alternative, then (Y) takes on the value of the wealth to be gained by divorcing Mrs. X. From table 4.1 the value of (Y) should then be set equal to the expected monetary value of divorce such that Y = -\$495,000. Assuming that the values of (G) and (f) remain unchanged and that the subjective probability of apprehension remains (p) = 0.2, the mathematical model indicates that homicide (H_j) is also a rational choice in that

$$H_j = H_j(EU_{hj} - EU_{lj})$$
$$= \$2,500,000 + \$495,000$$
$$= \$2,995,000$$

Based on the expected gains in personal wealth, Mr. X should now be even more interested in considering the murder of Mrs. X. Consequently, if Mr. X appears to be making the legitimate choice of divorcing Mrs. X prior to her murder the authorities should suspect Mr. X's very likely involvement in the business-like murder of his spouse.

The Effect of Perfect Information

When enforced secrecy and highly experienced hit-men are provided "free" to Mr. X in exchange for control of Mr. X and is insider information the expected gains in efficiency and level of information (degree of certainty) is so great that optimization is possible. Now the probability of apprehension is (p) = 0.0. Although decisions are not being made under strict conditions of risk, the format of the SEU model can still be used. Thus we have

$$EU_{hj} = U_j(G_j)$$
$$= \$5,000,000$$

$$EU_{lj} = U_j(Y_j)$$
$$= \$500,000$$

$$H_j = H_j(EU_{hj} - EU_{lj})$$
$$= U_j(G_j) - U_j(Y_j)$$
$$= \$4,500,000$$

The gains in efficiency and level of information simplify the decision process greatly. Whether the homicide alternative (H_j) is rational or not depends only on $H_j = U(G_j) - U(Y_j)$. The simplified single equation form of the mathematical model is probably more descriptive of the actual decision processes of business-like murders in which secrecy is enforced and highly efficient hit-men are used.[8] Assuming that "take no action" (status quo) is the next best legitimate alternative, the value of perfect information (or, equivalently, the highly experienced hit-men and partnership with organized crime) to Mr. X is equal to $H_j = U(G_j) - U(Y_j) =$

$5,000,000 - $500,000 = $4,500,000. This is a gain of $2,500,000 (that is, $4,500,000 - $2,000,000) over the expected value of the less experienced hit-men. Thus making a deal with Mr. Z's criminal organization also appears rational.

SEU and the Criminal Organization

The same three-equation model can be applied to Mr. Z's criminal organization. For the criminal organization, (G) represents the gains in wealth from homicide and (Y) represents the wealth gains from the criminal organization's next best alternative. Of course, (Y) is now more likely to be an illegitimate activity. Since the criminal organization can always enforce secrecy and can obtain the best hit-men available it considers that the subjective probability of apprehension is $p = 0.0$. The criminal organization (C) must then perceive the value of homicide (H_c) to be (H_c) = U(G) - U(Y) > 0 in order for Mrs. X's murder to be the best choice. If (Y) represents the gains from a relatively good alternative to murdering Mrs. X then (H_c) = U(G) - U(Y) ≤ 0 is more likely to be true. If (H_c) ≤ 0 the criminal organization will not offer the "free" hit-men to Mr. X and will seek the gains from alternative (Y).

On the other hand, as the gains from alternative (Y) diminish, so do Mrs. X's chances. For example, a criminal organization under heavy government scrutiny or investigation over activities that involve alternative (Y) might actually assign a negative monetary value to U(Y).[9] In this case, even if the value assigned by the criminal organization to U(G) is zero, this would create (H_c) = U(G) + U(Y) > 0. In this example U(G) would be zero if it became known to the police that the criminal organization was involved in Mrs. X's murder. Such information would not increase the probability of apprehension (p), however, if it is not a sufficient basis for issuing an arrest warrant.

In summary, if (p) = 0.0, U(Y) < 0, and U(G) ≥ 0, then (H_c) > 0 always results and the criminal organization would be acting rationally and optimally if it entered into a partnership with Mr. X. Therefore, it is possible that the criminal organization could be rationally involved in Mrs. X's murder even if it never realized any wealth gains (G). If U(G) is assigned a value that is greater than zero, a more likely case, the monetary value of homicide (H_c) to the criminal organization would be even greater.

SUGGESTED READINGS

1. Becker, G. "Crime and Punishment: An Economic Approach," *Journal of Political Economy* (March-April, 1968): 169-217.

2. Ehrlich, I. "The Deterrent Effect of Capital Punishment: A Question of Life and Death," *Journal of Political Economy* (June, 1975): 397-417.

CHAPTER 5
APPREHENSION RISK SENSITIVITY

The assumed risk preferring behavior of business-like murderers is analyzed in this chapter. Murder demand curves are derived from the risk preferring offender's utility function for wealth and the constrained utility-maximization model. The relatively greater sensitivity to apprehension risk assumed to be exhibited by business-like murderers suggests that criminal justice system resource allocations may be less than optimal. Moreover, homicide data appears to support this conclusion.

THE RISK-SEEKING HOMICIDE OFFENDER

An offender's attitude toward risk and the responsiveness of an offender's behavior to changes in risk are important to the theory of murder as a business decision. When conditions of risk are assumed as in the subjective expected utility (SEU) model, it implies that the offender is willing to take a gamble for greater wealth in exchange for a smaller amount of certain wealth. In effect, the business-like murderer "buys" risk with the homicide decision just as he or she would by betting on a horse race. A business-like murderer that is willing to buy risk through the murder choice is said to prefer risk over this range of his or her utility function. It will be shown that homicide offenders who have a preference for risk are relatively more sensitive to changes in the perceived risk of apprehension.

In contrast to buying risk, a risk-averse person can avoid or "sell" risk by purchasing insurance. The purchase of insurance simply transfers the risk to the insurer. However, even a risk-averse a homicide offender cannot sell homicide risk because there is no "insurance policy" against any of the risks associated with the murder choice.[1]

Under the assumed conditions of risk, the relative importance of apprehension, conviction, and punishment risks have been determined by Isaac Ehrlich (1975) in his study on the deterrent effect of capital punishment.[2] In this study the partial elasticities of the expected utility from murder with respect to the event probabilities in table 4.2 are shown to be ranked in descending order of importance as $\ni Pa > \ni Pc|a > \ni Pe|c > 0$.[3] These partial elasticities show the percentage effect on an offender's expected utility of murder from a 1 percent change in the subjective probability or conditional probability. Ehrlich (1975) suggests that this ranking implies that the more general the event or consequence is, the greater is the deterrent effect. Thus the risk of apprehension (Pa) has the greatest deterrent effect, assuming that the other two probabilities are held constant. Similarly, the conviction effect (Pc|a) has the next most important deterrent effect and the punishment effect (Pe|c) has the smallest deterrent effect. The statistical significance and the relative strength of these three deterrent effects are supported by Ehrlich's (1975) empirical results.

The relative importance of apprehension risk sensitivity can also be derived from the three-equation subjective expected utility (SEU) model developed in Chapter 4. Referring to equation 4.1, equal and offsetting percentage changes in apprehension risk (p) and the level of punishment (f) will not change expected utility (EU). This can be seen by taking the expected value of homicide gains (G) in equation 4.1 such that $E(G) = p(G - f) + (1 - p)G = G - pf$. For multiplicative terms like (pf), a positive(negative) %Δp minus(plus) an equal %Δf is approximately equal to zero. However, the negative of the partial derivatives for (p) and (f) and their mean values from equation 4.1 gives the elasticity formulas in which equal percentage changes can be compared.[4]

$$(-\partial UE/\partial p)(p/U) > (-\partial UE/\partial f)(f/U) \tag{5.1}$$

$$[U(G) - U(G - f)] (p/U) > pU'(G - f)(f/U) \tag{5.2}$$

$$[U(G) - U(G - f)]/f > U'(G - f). \tag{5.3}$$

The term on the left in equation (5.3) is the average change in utility between G and (G - f) and the term on the right is the rate of change in the utility of (G - f). For $f > 0$ and preferences for risk (defined as $U(G)" > 0$), the term on the left is greater than the term on the right. Thus equation 5.1 shows that an increase in apprehension risk (p) will change expected utility more than an equal percentage increase in punishment (f). How much more is not clear? For risk-averse offenders (defined as $U(G)" < 0$) the term on the right is greater and an increase in (f) will change expected utility more than an equal percentage increase in (p). Again, the magnitude of the difference cannot be determined. Risk neutral offenders (defined as $U(G)" = 0$) are influenced equally by changes in either (p) or (f).

Two examples may help illustrate the magnitude of the effect that an increase in apprehension risk (p) can have on the behavior of rationally motivated criminal offenders. The first example is based on the fact that the Pinkerton detectives solved many railroad robberies during the decade of the 1960s. This substantially increased the risk of apprehension for railroad robberies. Consequent to the increase in the apprehension risk for railroad robberies, many railroad robbers (for example, Butch Cassidy and the Sundance Kid) are thought to have moved to South America where the risk of apprehension (p) was considered to be relatively lower. There is no evidence that the probability of conviction or the level of punishment (f) for railroad robberies changed substantially during this period of time. The significance of the effect of the increase in apprehension risk (p) suggests that the relocated railroad robbers were risk-seekers. A second and more recent example is based on survey data provided by professional fisherman.[5] This study showed that professional fishermen, who can be assumed to be making rational, business-like decisions about whether to engage in illegal fishing, tend to also be more sensitive to changes in the risk of apprehension (p) than in punishment (f). Though obviously not murderers, these professional fishermen are clearly taking a gamble for relatively greater profits when they choose to fish illegally. Thus they too are indicated to be risk-seekers.

Additional Factors Suggesting The Importance of Risk

In the hypothetical examples of business-like murder in Chapter 4 it was clearly shown that planning, information, enforced secrecy, and organizational specialization are factors likely to reduce the risk of apprehension (p). Consequently, these factors appear to contribute significantly to the offender's objective (that is, the expected monetary value of wealth gains) in the case of murder as a business decision. The effect on the offender's expected utility is consistent with the fact that avoiding apprehension is a generally encompassing event that eliminates the occurrence of other conditional events that would reduce offender utility.

Rational calculation about homicide consequences along the time dimension also suggests that apprehension may carry relatively more weight in decisions than consequences that are farther removed in time from the homicide event such as conviction and punishment. The relevance of intertemporal effects obviously depends on whether the offender is discounting the value of future consequences. As it turns out, younger criminal offenders, who also commit a large number and proportion of homicides, tend to heavily discount future consequences.[6] Thus, even younger and less experienced homicide offenders, who probably tend to also seek wealth gains, are likely to be concerned with the more immediate risk of apprehension (p).

Although it appears reasonable to assume that business-like murderers are the most sensitive to changes in the risk of apprehension (p), the magnitude of this effect is not clear. Moreover, it is not clear how such an effect would become evident in terms of changes in individual behaviors. These are important considerations because the cost of increasing apprehension risk (p) and the conditional risks of conviction and punishment and the level of punishment (f) are very unlikely to all be equal. If, in the case of business-like murderers, increasing apprehension risk (p) is very costly relative to increasing (f), for example, then net benefits may actually favor increases in (f) over increases in (p).

The Risk-Seeking Utility Function and the Murder Demand Curve

Demand curves have a negative slope because price (marginal cost) is assumed to be inversely related to the quantity demanded of a given good in a given period of time, all else held constant. The downward slope can be explained by either the income and substitution effects or by diminishing marginal utility. For example, the demand curves for speeding in figure 3.1 sloped downward because it was assumed that beyond some point each mph of increased speed would provide less and less marginal utility to the speeder. The demand for speed curve will have a negative slope and remain in the positive quadrant as long as each mph of speed generates positive yet diminishing marginal utility. Moreover, all crime demand curves are expected to have negative slopes regardless of risk preferences.

The utility function associated with assumed diminishing marginal utility and a negatively sloped demand curve must be concave from below as in figure 1.2. The utility function simply summarizes the relationship between the total utility gained from an act (such as consumption or speeding) and the total quantity consumed (units of a good or mph of speeding) in a given period of time, all else held constant. The assumption of diminishing marginal utility means that total utility increases with each unit of quantity but at a diminishing rate. In other words, the slope of the total utility curve is positive and decreasing. This makes the utility function concave when viewed from below.

As previously indicated, a business-like murder decision is made by a decision maker who prefers to take a gamble for potentially greater wealth than the gains in wealth that would result a sure bet. The willingness to gamble rather than to accept the gains from a sure bet indicates that the decision maker prefers to take risks. The (von Neumann-Morgenstern) utility function associated with a preference for risk is one with increasing marginal utility for each unit of "wealth" sought. Increasing marginal utility for wealth serves is the inducement for the decision maker to trade away a choice (C_1) that would result in sure gains in wealth for a choice (C_2) that involves a gamble for greater gains in wealth. A risk-seeking business-like murderer who is assumed to seek primarily wealth gains has a von Neumann-Morgenstern utility function that is convex from below as in figure 5.1. So that the two choices (C_1 and C_2) in figure 5.1 will be relevant to the hypothetical business-like murder decision in Chapter 4, let sure choice C_1 be that the decision maker "takes no action" against his spouse while risky choice C_2 involves committing the planned murder of his spouse. Using apprehension risk (p) to represent the probability of receiving wealth gains (G) from either the "take no action" choice or the homicide table 5.1 indicates that the two choices can be shown to have the same expected value in that SEU = G_0 for both choices. The choices are set to the same SEU by allowing the risk or apprehension (p) = 0.5 for the unfavorable and favorable outcomes (gains G_1 and G_2) from the risky homicide choice (C_2).

Table 5.1
SEU for Risky and Sure Outcomes

Choices				SEU
C_1 (Sure Outcome)	$= p(G_0)$	$= 1.0(G_0)$		$= G_0$
C_2 (Risky Outcome)	$= p(G_1 + G_2)$	$= 0.5(G_1 + G_2)$		$= G_0$

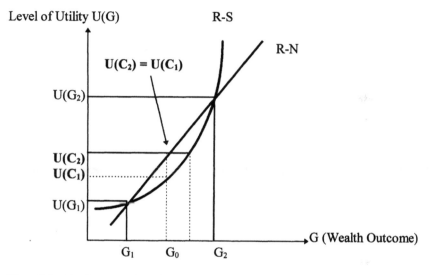

Fig. 5.1. Preferences for Risk. Indifference or neutrality toward risky and sure choices is reflected on the straight line utility function R-N where the offender receives the same level of utility in that $U(C_2) = U(C_1)$ from either the gamble or the sure bet. Even though the expected value of both choices (C_1 and C_2) is the same (see table 5.1), the level of utility from the risky choice C_2 must be greater than the level of utility from the sure choice C_1 in order for the offender to be induced to take the gamble. $U(C_2) > U(C_1)$ occurs only on the convex (from below) utility function R-S that reflects risk-seeking behavior.

When the straight line, risk-neutral utility function R-N in figure 5.1 describes the decision maker's attitude towards risk the utility of both choices is the same (that is, $U(C_1) = U(C_2) = G_0$). Given that the expected value of each choice is the same, risk-neutrality reflects an indifference on the part of the decision maker between the sure choice (C_1) and the gamble involving the risky choice (C_2). On the other hand, when the risk-seeking utility function R-S describes the decision maker's attitude towards risk, the utility of the risky choice is greater than the utility of the sure choice (that is, $U(C_2) > G_o = U(C_1)$). The convex utility function R-S clearly indicates that the decision maker would willingly exchange sure gains (G_o) for a gamble for possibly greater wealth gains. Since table 5.1 indicates that the SEU of both choices is the same only the decision maker's attitude toward risk provides a basis for the decision maker to choose the gamble.

Since the level of utility U(G) in figure 5.1 reflects the total utility from units of wealth gained in a given period of time, marginal utility is simply the slope of the total utility function at any given point. A less precise statement of this is that the average marginal utility over a segment of the utility function U(G) can be calculated as MU = ΔTU/ΔW (i.e., rise over run). More precisely, at any given point on the utility function marginal utility (MU) is the first derivative U'(G). For the risk-seeking utility function R-S, the slope of the concave utility function U(G) is clearly positive so that marginal utility is positive (or, equivalently, U'(G) > 0). Increasing marginal utility (concavity) is indicated by the positive second derivative U''(G) > 0. Since the choices of business-like murderers are assumed to reflect preferences for risk, the demand curve for murders committed as if they were a business decision should reflect increasing marginal utility for increasing quantities of wealth gains (G). By letting marginal utility equal marginal expected benefits (MEB) figure 5.2 shows the expected relationship between marginal utility and wealth gains (G). Notice that the two MEB curves slope upward.

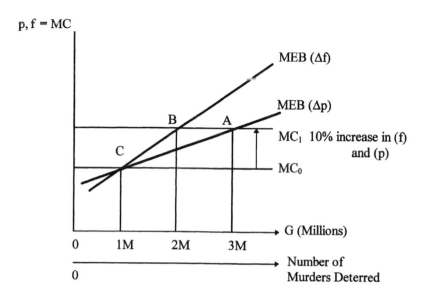

Fig. 5.2. MEB Curves for Murder as a Business Decision. When offenders prefer risk increasing marginal utility (MEB) is directly related to homicide gains (G). The marginal decision costs include the two criminal justice system controlled variables (p) and (f) and it is assumed that all else is held constant. A 10% increase in apprehension risk (p) deters more homicides (or, equivalently, wealth gains) than does an equal percentage increase in punishment (f).

Only the criminal justice system variables (p) and (f) are included in figure 5.2 and in the corresponding murder demand curves in figure 5.3 as marginal cost variables. The relevant marginal cost variables can be determined by substituting the expected utilities of homicide and legitimate alternatives into equation (4.3) where $H_j = H_j(EU_{hj} - EU_{lj})$. This results in

$$H_j = H_j [p_j U_j(G_j - f_j) + (1-p_j)U_j(G_j) - U_j(Y_j)] > 0. \qquad (5.4)$$

In equation (5.4) the relevant variables are indicated to be (p), (f), (G), and (Y) and it is assumed that $\partial H/\partial p < 0$, $\partial H/\partial f < 0$, $\partial H/\partial Y < 0$, and $\partial H/\partial G > 0$. Given that $H_j > 0$ is required for the homicide to be the best choice, the partial derivatives indicate that increases in any of the three variables apprehension risk (p), level of punishment (f), and opportunity cost (Y), all else held constant, will decrease the likelihood that homicide (H_j) will be the best (or even a rational) choice. On the other hand, increases in wealth gains (G) will increase (H_j).

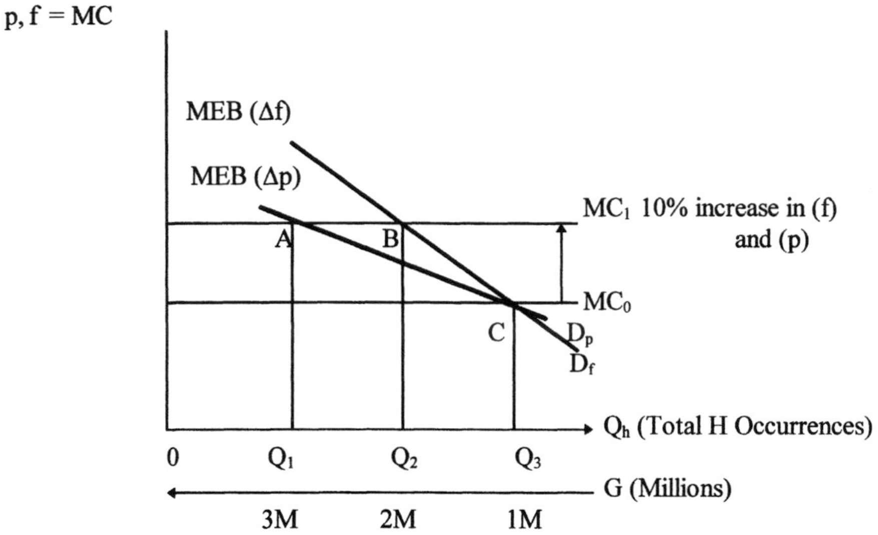

p, f = MC

MEB (Δf)

MEB (Δp)

MC_1 10% increase in (f) and (p)

A   B

MC_0

C D_p

D_f

Q_h (Total H Occurrences)

0   Q_1 Q_2 Q_3

G (Millions)

3M   2M   1M

Fig. 5.3. Demand Curves for Murder as a Business Decision. Figure 5.3 shows total occurrences of business-like murders (H) in a given period of time. Holding all else constant, the increases in (p) and (f) deter murders and produce downward sloping murder demand curves. Increases in apprehension risk (p) are expected to deter more business-like murders than an equal percentage increase in the level of punishment (f). Homicides where MEB > MC still occur or, equivalently, remain undeterred.

The legitimate opportunity cost variable (Y) is not included in figures 5.2 and 5.3 because the effect that a percentage change in legitimate opportunity cost (Y) would have is itself a function of the offender's age and age is not included as a parameter in equation (5.4). Regarding age, James Q. Wilson indicates that policies directed at increasing job skills or employment opportunities (that is, increasing Y) are most likely to be successful in deterring first-time, novice offenders and least likely to succeed for those who have already embarked on a career in crime.[7] Thus when a murder is considered by organized crime (that is, older, professional offenders) legitimate opportunity cost (Y) is probably an irrelevant decision parameter.

The partial derivative for gains (G) in the homicide function (5.4) indicates that (G) should be plotted as directly related to the marginal expected benefit (MEB) curves in figure 5.2. Also, increases in (p) and (f) should increase homicides (or gains) deterred (that is, reduce homicide occurrences).

In figure 5.3 the MEB curves are reversed and drawn as diminishing MEB (that is, murder demand) curves. The deterrence variables apprehension risk (p) and punishment (f) are plotted as inversely related to homicide gains (G) or, equivalently, to homicide occurrences (H). Thus the deterrence variables cause the "murder as a business decision" demand curves to slope downwards, all else held constant.

The two marginal cost variables controlled by the criminal justice system are the probability of apprehension (p) and the level of punishment (f). As previously indicated, risk-seeking homicide offenders are expected to be more sensitive to changes in (p) than (f). Thus a 10% increase in (p) deters more homicides than a 10% increase in (f). For example, Figures 5.2 and 5.3 indicate that a 10% increase in (p) will deter all business-decision homicides for which wealth related gains (G) is less than three million dollars. However, the same 10% increase in (f) will only deter business-decision homicides in which (G) is less than two million dollars.

MURDER DEMAND AND OPTIMAL CHOICES

The constrained-utility maximization model can be used to illustrate optimal choices when the decision maker is assumed to prefer risk. The same downward sloping murder demand curves can also be derived. In the graphical representation of the constrained-utility maximization model there must be two goods or action choices. For the business-like murderer, the two "goods" (choices) can be the inverses of the two "bads" apprehension risk (p) and the level of punishment (f). All other relevant factors must be assumed constant.

In figure 5.4 (1/p) and (1/f) serve as the two goods. The indifference curves in figure 5.4 represent the willingness to trade away one good (choice) for the other while maintaining the same level of utility or wealth gains. For murder as a business decision, the offender is assumed to prefer risk and be relatively more sensitive to a given percentage change in (p) than in (f). Accordingly, changes in (1/p) will effect the offender's level of utility (wealth gains) more than equal percentage changes in (1/f) and the corresponding indifference curves should reflect this. In the extreme, an offender that is completely insensitive to changes in punishment (f) would perceive good (1/f) as a "neuter" and the indifference curve would actually be horizontal to the (1/f) axis. Indifference curves that are relatively flatter against the (1/f) axis reflect that the offender is willing to trade away the risk related good (1/p) only for substantially greater amounts of (1/f) in order to maintain the same level of utility (wealth gains). Indifference curves that reflect a preference for risk will generate an indifference curve mapping that expands and contracts more along the purely risk related good's (1/p) axis. Thus the income (or wealth gains) expansion path of the assumed risk-seeking business-like murderer indicates a preference for "buying" the risk related (1/p) good.

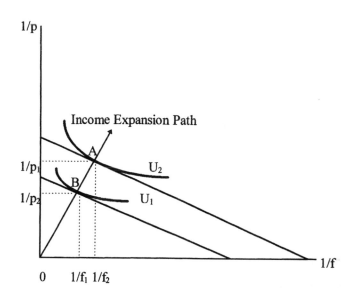

Fig. 5.4. Optimal Choices for the Business-Like Murderer. For business-like murderers who are assumed to prefer risk, optimal choices lie along an income (wealth gains) expansion path that favors the (1/p) axis. Equal percentage changes in apprehension risk (p) and punishment (f) produces relatively greater wealth effects for the (1/p) good as can be seen by $(1/p_1 - 1/p_2) > (1/f_2 - 1/f_1)$.

The slope of the budget constraints in figure 5.4 is equal to -1/2. This reflects the assumption that good (1/p) is twice as "expensive" to the business-like murderer as good (1/f). This is because risk sensitivity and utility maximization suggests that business-like murderers are likely to devote relatively more resources towards reducing the risk of apprehension (p). In figure 5.4, exactly twice as many resources are devoted to reducing (p). For highly experienced or professional business-like murderers who may place an even greater emphasis on reducing (p), the slope of the budget constraint may actually be much less than -1/2.

The budget constraints in figure 5.4 are parallel straight lines that shift horizontally inward or outward for equal percentage changes in the variables (p) and (f). Changes in (p) and (f) is analogous to equal percentage changes in the prices of consumer goods (1/p) and (1/f) while assuming wealth gains (G), analogous to consumer income, is held constant. By holding wealth gains from homicide constant, an equal percentage increase in (p) and (f) would decrease the ability to consume (chosen) goods (1/p) and (1/f) by the same amount. In this way "price" increases deter the homicide choice. If homicide gains (G) were increased the same as (p) and (f) the offender could "afford" to buy the same amount of goods (1/p) and (1/f) by devoting more resources to reducing apprehension risk (p) and the corresponding relevance of punishment (f).

Given that equal percentage increases in (p) and (f) cause the budget line to shift inward but do not change its slope, figure 5.4 indicates that equal percentage increases in both (p) and (f) decrease in the level of utility (wealth gains) from (U_2) to (U_1). Accordingly, the optimal choice changes from A to B and there is clearly a greater wealth effect for the business-like murderer along the (1/p) axis. The decrease in total utility or wealth gains (G) due to a given percentage increase in (p) can be thought of as corresponding the flatter (more elastic) murder demand (or MEB) curve in figure 5.3 while the equal percentage increase in (f) corresponds to the steeper murder demand (or MEB) curve.

A technical problem that arises from attempting to derive murder demand curves from the constrained-utility maximization model is that optimal choices assume perfect information, however, the murder demand (MEB) curves in figure 5.3 reflect subjective expected utility. Subjective expected utility implies that the decision maker has less than perfect information. To resolve this conflict the "optimal" choices A and B in figure 5.4 should be considered as only the "best choices."

DETERRENCE PRODUCTION

Holding all else constant, optimal and efficient choices in the production of apprehension risk (p) and the level of punishment (f) by units of the criminal justice system can be determined. A two-output (p and f) and one-input (aggregate resources) model is illustrated in figure 5.5. For the crime of murder, as opposed to speeding, the level of punishment (f) is unlikely to be a simple monetary fine that is relatively easy to produce. Instead, the level of punishment (f) for murder, especially for a business-like murder, is likely to be imprisonment or execution and be much more costly to produce. Like the level of punishment (f), the risk of apprehension (p) for business-like homicide offenders will also be costly to produce. This is because risk-sensitive business-like homicide offenders are expected to make every attempt to reduce apprehension risk (p) to as near zero as possible. Because criminal resources in business-like murders are expected to be aimed more at reducing apprehension risk (p) than the level of punishment (f), it is assumed that a given level of (p) is about twice as expensive to produce as the same level of (f).[8] Accordingly, the production possibility frontier in figure 5.5 indicates that for a given level of resources the criminal justice system has the ability to efficiently produce about twice the amount of output (f). The production possibility frontier will be bowed outward significantly because, for homicide, the resources used in the production of apprehension risk (p) and punishment (f) are highly specialized. Consequently these resources cannot be easily substituted for each other without incurring large opportunity costs. For business-like homicide offenders, the production possibility frontier in figure 5.5 represents the maximum or efficient level of deterrence outputs (p) and (f) for a given level of criminal justice system resources (or cost). The maximum level of apprehension risk production and the maximum level of punishment for business-like murders have been set arbitrarily at $p = 0.5$ and $f = 30$ years served, respectively. It is assumed that the given level of criminal justice system resources is socially optimal.

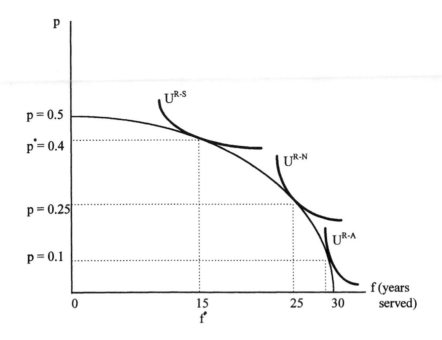

Fig. 5.5. Deterrence Production for Murder as a Business Decision. For business-like homicide offenders who are assumed to be risk-seekers (R-S), the tangency point between the production possibility frontier and social utility function U^{R-S} reflects the socially optimal output combination of p* = 0.4 and f* = 15 years served. Tangency's between the production possibility frontier and the social utility functions U^{R-N} and U^{R-A} reflect the optimal output combinations of p and f for risk-neutral (R-N) and risk-averse (R-A) offenders, respectively.

The social utility curves in figure 5.5 reflect the rate that the criminal justice system can substitute one output for the other and maintain the same level of deterrence. For risk sensitive business-like homicide offenders, changes in apprehension risk (p) have a greater deterrent effect than an equal percentage change in the level of punishment (f). Consequently, the social utility curves for risk-seeking homicide offenders should reflect a low rate of willingness to trade (p) for (f). Homicide offenders classified as risk-neutral and risk-averse, have social utility curves that are rotated clockwise, respectively, to become steeper and reflect increasing sensitivity to changes in (f) relative to changes in (p). The point of tangency between the criminal justice system production possibility frontier and the relevant social utility curve reflects the optimal and efficient combination of (p) and (f) to be produced. For assumed risk-seeking, business-like homicide offenders the optimal and efficient combination of outputs (p) and (f) is indicated to be p* = 0.4 and f* = 15 years served.

When business-like murder is committed by highly experienced and professional offenders, the actual probability of apprehension and the level of punishment appears to be much less than p* = 0.4 and f* = 15 years. For example, page A-4 of the June 13, 1976, edition of the ARIZONA REPUBLIC reports "8 cases since 1955, mob hits here all unsolved." Concerning professionally committed homicides or business-like murders, observations such as these are fairly common. This suggests that, with respect to the most experienced offenders, most police units probably operate well within their production possibility frontiers or, equivalently, produce deterrence for business-like murder very inefficiently. On the other hand, less experienced business-like offenders are apprehended much more frequently.

The crime mixes of most police units is likely to involve very few business-like murders. Moreover, a low probability of apprehension for business-like murders would translate into a much higher probability of apprehension for risk-neutral and risk-averse decision makers.[9] Risk-averse murderers commit unplanned, probably emotionally motivated homicides in which their concern is more likely to be on the level of punishment (f) rather than on reducing apprehension risk (p).[10] On the average, this should result in a greater amount of evidence that can be used against the offender. Figure 5.4 indicates that the optimal level of punishment (f) should be much higher than it actually is in the common case of risk-averse homicide offenders if social utility (deterrence) is to be produced efficiently by the criminal justice system.

Data indicate that the mean time served (in months) in State Prisons for murder and non-negligent manslaughter before first release has fallen significantly since 1960. It fell from (f) = 121.4 (10.1 years) in 1960 to (f) = 84.0 (7 years) in

1991.[11] Moreover, the percentage of offenses known to the police that are cleared by arrest indicates that the probability of apprehension (p) for the aggregate of all murder and non-negligent manslaughter has also fallen since 1960. It fell from (p) = 92.3 percent in 1960 to (p) = 67.2 percent in 1991. Decreases in both (p) and (f), as opposed to trade-offs among them, suggest inefficient deterrence production that occurs inside the production possibility frontier. Moreover, assuming that most homicide offenders are risk-averse, the decrease in the level of punishment (f) is completely inconsistent with achieving the optimal level of social utility for homicide deterrence.

It should also be pointed out that the reduction in apprehension risk (p) for homicide offenders that are predominantly risk-averse suggests an even lower level of apprehension risk (p) for professional, business-like homicide offenders. This increases the number of opportunities to commit murder as a business decision. If crime mixes reflect an increase in the proportion of homicides classified as business-like, the consequences could be very dire. This is especially true for smaller police jurisdictions with less experienced investigators.[12]

Criminal justice system deterrence production inefficiency is indicated by decreases in apprehension risk (p) and punishment (f), all else held constant. If economic theory is correct less deterrence should lead to more homicides over this same period of time. The data indicate that in 1960 the crime rate (per 100,000) for murder and non-negligent manslaughter was 5.1. By 1991 this rate had nearly doubled to 9.8. Perhaps some of the increase in the overall homicide crime rate is also due to an increase in the number and proportion of business-like homicides. In any case, the predictions of economic theory appear to stand unrefuted.

SUGGESTED READINGS

1   Furlong, W. "The Deterrent Effect of Regulatory Enforcement in the Fishery," *Land Economics* (February 1991): 116-129.

2.   Wilson, J. Q. *THINKING ABOUT CRIME* (rev. ed.), 1983.

3.   Marché, G. "The Production of Homicide Solutions: An Empirical Analysis," *The American Journal of Economics and Sociology* (October 1994): 385-401.

4.   Clark, J. R., and D. R. Lee, "Sentencing Laffer Curves, Political Myopia, and Prison Space," *Social Science Quarterly* 77 (June 1996): 245-255.

CHAPTER 6

THE CHARACTERISTICS OF RATIONALLY MOTIVATED

HOMICIDES

This chapter discusses several limitations in existing criminal profiles and overcomes these limitations to develop a new and improved profile of rationally motivated homicides. The new profile is based on theoretical material developed in earlier chapters and is rigorously tested using actual homicide data.[1]

THE NEED FOR A NEW PROFILE

The FBI develops psychological or criminal profiles in an effort to help apprehend highly mobile serial-killers. Unfortunately, these profiles appear to have several significant limitations and have not been shown to be productive. One of the major limitations of existing criminal profiles is that they have a very narrow focus. For the broader set of rationally motivated homicides, there are currently no criminal profiles. This deficiency is addressed by developing a criminal profile of rationally motivated homicides that is consistent with the subjective expected utility (SEU) models in earlier chapters.

An additional benefit from developing the new profile for business-like murderers is that the theoretical material developed earlier can now be tested against real world data. For example, it has been argued that rationally motivated, business-like homicide offenders tend to be highly sensitive to changes in the risk of apprehension and have preferences for wealth gains. Hypotheses such as these need to be tested before they can be fully relied upon.

A new criminal profile for rationally motivated business-like homicides may also aid investigators in differentiating between murder as a business decision and other types of homicides. This may increase investigator productivity in the case of murder as a business decision.

Limitations of Existing Profiles

Criminal profiles consist merely of hypotheses about what the actual characteristics of an unknown offender might be. A criminal profile can, therefore, be tested against reality and refuted. A major deficiency of existing criminal profiles is that they are often refuted in real world applications. Implications from movies and television aside, it is a fact that there is little or no data indicating that criminal profiles, such as those developed and used by the FBI, are actually effective in apprehending actual suspects. For example, Anthony Pinizzotto and Norman Finkel (1990) found, for a homicide in which the actual offender was already known, that detectives, psychologists, undergraduates and profilers were equally accurate, or inaccurate, in identifying the true offender.[2]

The lack of effectiveness of existing criminal profiles may be due to several reasons. These include the lack of a theoretical foundation, a limited range of applicability among homicide types, and the use of biased offender data. Because they lack a theoretical foundation, criminal profiles have no comprehensive behavior theory, decision theory, or any other theoretical basis upon which the characteristics of an unknown offender can be analyzed, hypothesized, assumed, or predicted. This is obviously a series deficiency. It means that the foundation of a criminal profile is pure subjectivity.

The predictable attempts to reduce the probability of apprehension by business-like murderers will cause business-like murderers to be underrepresented in offender data. This is important because Ronald Turco points out that existing criminal profile data is based on the collected demographic characteristics of known homicide offenders and data from interviews with serial killers.[3] Specifically, the use of biased data limits profiles to the types of crimes that are characterized by bizarre behavior and crime scenes in which there is evidence of psychopathology.[4] Therefore, it seems reasonable to expect that the use of existing criminal profiles in cases involving business-like homicides would likely be to throw the police off the trail of the actual offender or offenders.

Biased data would tend to reinforce attitudes and believes about crime and criminal behavior. Attitudes and beliefs by police will be reflected as preferences for homicide offenders with certain demographic and behavior characteristics. Business-like murderers may simply take advantage of attitudes and beliefs (preferred characteristics) by using them to reduce the probability of apprehension. For example, offenders may find that staging crime scenes so as to appear to be characterized by bizarre behavior would be effective. It seems obvious that this type of crime scene staging should be expected. In fact, Ronald Turco suggests that some offenders may actually read appropriate materials to find out what law enforcement expects them to do so that they can deliberately fool the police.[5]

The effects of attitudes and beliefs on the part of law enforcement and deliberate attempts to fool the police by criminals will result in the reinforcement of homicide solution probabilities that differ among homicide types. Moreover, these probabilities may often be exemplified through the use of criminal profiles. This is because the subjective basis of criminal profiles would reflect the profiler's clinical experience with a biased set of apprehended offenders.

Another way of looking at existing criminal profiles and the way they are used is based on the fact that criminal profile hypotheses are merely extrapolations of past law enforcement experiences. In other words, past experience provides the subjective basis of a criminal profile. Thus the use of criminal profiles is somewhat analogous to driving a car in which the windshield and side windows are completely covered over so that the driver can only see out the review mirror. When the FBI uses a criminal profile to help identify a criminal suspect it is, in effect, driving such a car through society. Experienced and professional criminal offenders have a direct interest in what law enforcement does and they are likely to carefully avoid the FBI's speeding car. On the other hand, innocent and unwary citizens may occasionally be very significantly injured by the speeding car (profile) when it suddenly approaches them.

There is no reason to believe that rational expectations do not apply to criminal offenders. The rational expectation's hypothesis is that individuals learn what government policies (usually fiscal and monetary policies) to expect and then change their behavior in order to take advantage of any opportunities presented by these policies. Consistent with the *fallacy of composition* the collective effect of individual actions may offset or nullify the intended effects of the government policy. For example, bond and stock holders anticipating short-run stimulative monetary policy might also expect a pick-up in inflation. Consequently they may begin to re-allocate their financial resources from lending in the financial markets to borrowing in real estate markets. This may nullify or off-set the intended decrease in short-run interest rates and the stimulative monetary policy. Criminals may behave similarly. For example, the criminal profile for drug smugglers is always changing. This is because drug smugglers learn what profiles the government is using and then, based upon rational expectations, use a smuggler that law enforcement officials will not suspect. In other words, the drug smugglers jump out of the way of the profiler.

The subjectivity of the driver (in applying the profile) suggests that just about anyone is at risk of becoming a homicide suspect. For example, the pipe bombing that occurred in Atlanta's Centennial Olympic Park on July 27, 1996, may be an example of this type of "reckless driving." Richard Jewell, the security guard who initially found the bomb, became the primary suspect through the application of an FBI "lone bomber" profile. However, Richard Jewell's lawyer indicated that his client did not have time to place a warning call that a bomb was about to go off and still get back to his security guard post and that his client does not appear to fit the profile very closely. The fact that it was physically impossible for Richard Jewell to have planted the bomb and that he did not fit the "lone bomber" profile illustrates the highly subjective nature and arbitrary application of criminal profiles. Richard Jewell was subsequently cleared as a suspect by the FBI but the application of the profile has significantly damaged the security guard's career and reputation. Perhaps it is unfortunate that it is so difficult for innocent citizens to recover damages from the FBI.

The limitations and deficiencies of criminal profiles suggest that there is a causal interaction between biased homicide offender data on the one hand and the limited applicability of criminal profiles and the attitudes and beliefs (or preferences) of law enforcement on the other hand. Moreover, any bias on the part of law enforcement that suggests that business-like homicide offenders are likely to be ignored as suspects suggests that there is a large "hole in the police dragnet" through which rationally motivated, business-like murderers can routinely pass.

Using an Economic Model as the Basis for a Criminal Profile

As it turns out, criminal profiles and economic theories or models have some characteristics in common. One characteristic is that criminal profiles and economic models make widely applicable behavioral assumptions. For example, economic models assume rational behavior and criminal profiles assume that the way people think directs their behavior.[6] Obviously, since the way people think cannot be observed it is necessary to make inferences from behavioral observations. For criminal profiles, inferences about the way people think are based on behaviors and demographic characteristics. Assuming that one then "knows" how someone else thinks particular actions (such as homicides) may then become more predictable. Similarly for economical models, the inference sought is that people act as if they are rationale. The inference of rationale behavior is warranted only when people tend to act in a manner that is consistent with the predictions of the economic model.

A second characteristic in common is that economic models and criminal profiles make assumptions about how and under what conditions any unobservable behavioral assertions will relate to reality. For example, economic models often assume that all other factors are held constant. This is the well known ceteris paribus assumption of partial equilibrium analysis. Criminal profiles, on the other hand, relate the behavioral assumption (that the way people think directs their behavior) to real objects by predicting particular demographic and behavior characteristics that are suggested by an unknown offender's hypothesized actions at a particular crime scene.

A third characteristic in common is that the hypotheses of economic models and criminal profiles can both be tested against reality and refuted. For either a criminal profile or economic theory, refutation is more likely when the subject of analysis is a particular individual. For example, if Mr. Jones is not in the bread market then the consumer model may not accurately predict how Mr. Jones will react to a change in the price of bread. On the other hand, the consumer model is accurate when predicting the marginal behavior of consumers as a whole. Similarly, criminal profiles cannot determine whether a given person committed a specific act at a specific time.[7] Unlike economic theory, however, it is not known whether criminal profiles can predict group behavior at the margin.

To summarize, economic models and criminal profiles have some important characteristics in common. Both are based on widely applicable behavioral assertions that are, in turn, systematically related to real objects. Also, they both make refutable predictions. Using an economic model to develop a criminal profile will also integrate a theoretical foundation and a comprehensive behavior theory into the profiling process. Thus it appears that there are sufficient justifications for using an economic model, such as the SEU model of murder as a business decision, as the theoretical basis for a criminal profile. The theoretical foundation and behavior theory should significantly limit the amount of subjectivity in the development and application of the profile and, thereby, limit the interrelated effects of attitudes, beliefs and biased data. Perhaps an economic based criminal profile will even be more effective in helping police solve crimes.

MODEL DEVELOPMENT

The mathematical model of subjective expected utility (SEU) consisting of the three equations (4.1), (4.2), and (4.3) provide the foundation for developing a criminal profile of rationally motivated homicide offenders. This model consisted of the following three equations

$$EU_{hj} = p_j U_j (G_j - f_j) + (1-p_j)U_j(G_j) \tag{6.1}$$

$$EU_{lj} = U_j(Y_j) \tag{6.2}$$

$$H_j = H_j(EU_{hj} - EU_{lj}). \tag{6.3}$$

Substituting for expected utility (EU) in (6.3) produces equation (6.4)

$$H_j = H_j [p_j U_j(G_j - f_j) + (1-p_j)U_j(G_j) - U_j(Y_j)] > 0 \tag{6.4}$$

which is the same as equation (5.4). Again, it is assumed that $\partial H/\partial p < 0$, $\partial H/\partial f < 0$, $\partial H/\partial Y < 0$, and $\partial H/\partial G > 0$.

Equation (6.4) says that offender (j), who is assumed rational, considers homicide (H_j) to be the best choice among the set of relevant (wealth gaining) alternatives if $H_j > 0$. Clearly homicide (H_j) is a function of the risk of apprehension (p), the level of punishment (f), the wealth related gains (G) and the legitimate opportunity cost (Y).

A more general form of equation (6.4) can be written as

$$HR = HR(p, f, G, Y). \tag{6.5}$$

In equation (6.5) it is also assumed that $\partial HR/\partial p < 0$, $\partial HR/\partial f < 0$, $\partial HR/\partial Y < 0$, and $\partial HR/\partial G > 0$. Equation (6.5) will serve as the basis for developing a criminal profile for murder as a business decision. The left hand term (HR) indicates a rationally motivated homicide. Equation (6.5) and the partial derivatives (which hold all other factors constant) indicate that whether a homicide is likely to be rationally motivated is inversely related to (p), (f) and (Y), and directly related to (G). Since the offender is expected to make every attempt to decrease apprehension risk (p) an increase in risk (p) means the homicide is less likely to be considered rational. Similarly, if punishment (f) and opportunity costs (Y) are increased, homicide (HR) is also less likely to be defined as rationally motivated. On the other hand, an increase in expected wealth gains (G) mean homicide (HR) is more likely to be rationally motivated.

Even if rationally motivated homicides (HR) include those that are committed by serial killers and political terrorists, all that is really required for equation (6.5) to represent business-like homicide is that a relatively high proportion of all rationally motivated homicide gains be wealth related. This appears likely to be so. The data used to estimate and test equation (6.5) indicate that approximately one-third of all homicides committed in the U. S. each year (that is, about 7,000 to 8,000) are rationally motivated. Estimates are that serial-killers commit about 200 to 300 homicides each year. If hate crimes[8] that result in homicide are included in the category of homicides committed by political terrorists, the number of homicides committed by political terrorists and serial-killers combined would probably average less than 1,000. This means that approximately 85% of all rationally motivated homicides are consistent with murder as a business decision.

Statistical Issues

There are two ways to estimate equation (6.5). One is to let (p), (f), (G), and (Y) be represented by proxy variables, such as their average rates, for some unit of observation such as a police jurisdiction. The dependent variable HR can simply be the total number of homicides that appear to be rationally motivated. Unfortunately, several significant statistical complications arise from using aggregated measures. For example, the left hand side variable would be associated with population and, hence, highly significant work-load effects on the production of apprehension risk (p). This creates the need to specify equation (6.5) as a simultaneous equation system in which some of the variables are endogenously determined. Once the simultaneous equation system is specified such that production is a dependent variable, the additional problem of production function nonseparability by crime type suggests that only aggregate measures of crime can be used to get unbiased estimates. In other words, in addition to solving homicides, police resources are used to solve other types of crimes.[9] There may also be production technology changes among different sized police units. Changes in technology shift cost and production functions and, thereby, decrease the meaningfulness of statistical estimates.[10]

In addition to creating specification and other estimation problems, an aggregated model is not very useful for developing a criminal profile for rationally motivated, business-like homicides. This is because proxy variables such as average jurisdictional values for (p), (f), (G), and (Y) would not provide detailed demographic characteristics that can be related to particular individual homicide offenders.

As it turns out, the statistical problems can be eliminated and the individually related demographic characteristics that are suitable for developing a criminal profile can be obtained by using individual homicide offender observations. Accordingly, this is the method used in this analysis.

For individual offender observations equation (6.5) can be re-written as

$$HR_{ij} = HR(p_{ij}, f_{ij}, G_i, Y_j). \tag{6.6}$$

In equation (6.6), the individual offender is (j) and each homicide incident is (i). The variables (p_{ij}), (f_{ij}), (G_i), and (Y_j), represent individualized decision parameter vectors. The decision parameter vectors (p_{ij}), (f_{ij}), (G_i), and (Y_j) are expected to be related to homicides defined to be rationally motivated (HR_{ij}).

Defining homicide (HR_{ij}) as rationally motivated is the same as assuming that offender (j) is acting rationally. The value of apprehension risk (p_{ij}) and the level of punishment (f_{ij}) depends on the jth offender and the ith homicide incident. The value of wealth gains (G_i) depends only on homicide event (i) and the value of the legitimate wealth gains alternative (Y_j) depends only on the jth offender. Values expected to be assigned to each decision parameter vector by offender (j) can be represented by real and observable factors that are unique to each offender (j) and homicide event (i). If the values for any of the variables (p_{ij}), (f_{ij}), and (Y_j) indicate increases and/or the values for (G_i) indicate a decrease, then homicide (Hr_{ij}) is less likely to be rationally motivated (or, equivalently, offender (j) is less likely to be acting rationally). In this way the decision parameter vectors become the hypothesized characteristics of a profile for rationally motivated homicides.

Defining Rationally Motivated Homicides

Regardless of whether aggregated or individualized observations are used (HR) must be defined for each observation. One way to define and designate homicide (HR) as either rationally motivated (true) or not rationally motivated (false) is to use a direct measure of motive. The data used to estimate equation (6.6) is the Uniform Crime Reports [United States]: Supplementary Homicide Reports, 1976-1983. Only the 1983 supplementary homicide report (SHR) data is used and it provides 21,128 non-negligent homicide offender observations.[11] Supplemental homicide reports (SHRs) are monthly reports submitted to the Federal Bureau of Investigation (FBI) by local law enforcement agencies participating in the FBI's Uniform Crime Reporting Program. Although the SHR data provides plenty of variables related to offenders and the decision parameter vectors (p_{ij}), (f_{ij}), (G_i), and (Y_j), the SHR data does not include any direct measure of motive. This is unfortunate. If the SHR data provided for the identification of specific motives (such as wealth gains) the dependent variable (HRij) could be changed to directly represent murder as a business decision.

The method used in this analysis to designate (HR) as either true or false is to use the definition of rational behavior and it's implications. Rational behavior is defined to involve only those actions or choices in which the decision maker is aware of the consequences. Decision consequences are either benefits or costs depending on whether they help or hinder the attainment of the decision maker's objective (preference). The definition of rational behavior does not require that a significant degree of consideration be given to consequences. Thus most homicides are likely to include some degree of rational behavior. In fact, there is empirical support for this assertion provided by criminologists in several studies. These studies indicate that some apparently impulsive assaults and homicides may be socially influenced and appear to reflect some degree of rational behavior on the part of the offender.[12] Whether rational calculation appears to be the predominant aspect of the offender's behavior that provides the motivation to commit the act of murder is the question to be answered in the designation of (HR) as either true or false. For individual offender observations (HRij) will be a discrete variable that takes on the value of 1 if it is true and 0 if it is not. This makes equation (6.6) a qualitative response model.

If it can be assumed that most homicides are characterized by some degree of awareness of the consequences, the extreme severity of homicide consequences also suggests that the motivation to homicidal action should be relatively powerful. Accordingly, powerful emotions or rational calculation would provide sufficient "springs to action." More specifically stated, powerful emotions or rational calculation would be sufficient to provide a motive, objective, or preference for which homicide may be among the relevant alternatives.

Generally, emotions play the role of prioritizing many objectives or preferences that are non-business related. In some cases, very strong and negative emotions such as hatred, jealousy, obsessive possessiveness, rejection, or vengefulness may arise from relationships between individuals. Emotions such as these may actually provide a sufficient motivation for one individual to murder another. Stated in this way, however, motivation is not necessarily equivalent to preferences or objectives. A more correct statement is that powerful negative emotions create a preference, objective, or motivation for an individual to relieve them in some manner. For some individuals, homicide may appear to be the best alternative among those available. Once the homicide or other alternatives are chosen and acted on the negative emotions are expected to be relieved.

Since emotions can prioritize preferences that can be gained through homicide and because rational behavior does not require extensive calculation, emotionally motivated homicides are subject to economic analysis. However, powerful emotions are not equivalent to rational calculation. Moreover, powerful emotions may impart a sense of urgency that causes the offender to act more rashly or impulsively when choosing among alternatives. This is especially true if the offender is taking illegal drugs.[13] This suggests that the amount of time the offender is able to devote to information processing and rational calculation prior to choosing the homicide alternative is constrained. In other words, an emotionally motivated homicide offender may tend to act (i.e., choose the homicide alternative) on less than perfect information and rational calculation may, therefore, tend to be more bounded or limited.

Relieving powerful negative emotions through homicide does not require that the offender remain unapprehended. Therefore, satisfying an emotionally determined objective or objectives through homicide may not require experience or significant rational calculation aimed at reducing the risk of apprehension. Moreover, the interpersonal focus of emotionally motivated homicides, coupled with a possible sense of urgency, may obviate the desire to involve additional homicide offenders or conspirators prior to and during the course of the event. In some cases the relief of the offender's specific emotionally based objective(s) may even require that he or she make it clear (at least to the victim) exactly who the offender is. This may make avoiding apprehension even less important to the offender.

It is reasonable to suggest that O. J. Simpson's status as an "acquitted murderer" serves as an example of the type of emotionally motivated homicide in which the offender wants to be identified--at least to the victim. It is well known that O. J. Simpson once stated that "if he killed Nicole it would be because he loved her too much." From this statement it is reasonable to infer that the desire to relieve powerful negative emotions such as obsessive possessiveness and rejection comprised the emotionally based objective of O. J. Simpson. He apparently considered homicide to be the best alternative to achieve his objective. The Simpson case also illustrates that an emotionally motivated homicide is likely to be a suboptimal choice in which the consequences of being in the "irrational zone" are forever clearly illustrated to the offender.[14]

Emotionally motivated homicides are different from murder as a business decision in which wealth gains are the objective. To achieve wealth gains the offender must not be identified, apprehended and convicted. Thus when wealth is sought, or is among the offenders' objectives, business-like rational calculation suggests time consuming planning or, at least, acquired experience aimed at reducing the risk of apprehension. The need to not be apprehended and the focus on an object such as wealth (as opposed to an interpersonal focus) suggests that powerful emotions would tend to play much less of a role prior to and during the course of a rationally motivated homicide event. Also, there is time to involve additional offenders so that gains from specialization can be achieved.

It is not being suggested that emotions and rational calculation are mutually exclusive. It is simply being argued that powerful emotions or rational calculation is likely to inhibit or constrain the role that the other plays in making a decision that involves a homicidal action choice. In those homicides where powerful emotions do not appear to be involved, it is assumed that the homicide choice was made on the basis of more extensive rational calculation.

The lack of an emotionally based objective does not rule out the possibility that some type of mental illness can provide an offender with a non-wealth related motive (objective or preference) that can be gained through the homicide alternative and that when the homicide choice is made it is based on extensive rational calculation. For example, psychological motives or objectives based on delusions or paranoid schizophrenia could, in some cases, be attained through a homicide. More extensive rational calculation, regardless of whether the objective is wealth or psychological (or a combination of the two) is especially important if the attainment of the objective(s) requires the offender to avoid apprehension. For example, David Berkowitz (the "Son of Sam") admitted killing on the basis of delusions. Consistent with the attainment of his psychological objectives (delusions) he avoided apprehension as a serial-killer. As a classic example of a paranoid schizophrenic, the alleged "Unabomber" Theodore Kaczynski appears to also be driven (probably on the basis of a mental illness) to gain psychological objectives involving distrust. As an objective, maximizing the gains of "distrust" (of technology, those related to it, the government, and relatives) can only occur if the "Unabomber" avoids apprehension. If thought of as a re-occurring emotion, the relief of "distrust" also requires repeated actions. Psychological objectives or motivations that can be gained only if the offender avoids apprehension suggest that homicidal choices are more likely to be made on the basis of extensive rational calculation.

One should note also that extensive rational calculation that decreases the risk of apprehension leads eventually to a homicide offender with extensive experience. In this sense, "extensive rational calculation" and "extensive experience" can be used interchangeably.

Psychologically based objectives can also motivate repeat homicide offenders (serial-killers) who tend to gain experience over time. Thus repeat homicide offenders such as serial-killers can be considered to choose the homicide alternative on the basis of more extensive rational calculation. Serial-killers also create a great deal of fascination -- with the public and with criminal investigators. In actual numbers, however, there are likely to be many more rationally motivated business-like murderers who have wealth related objectives. In other words, psychologically motivated serial-killers are rare but "in demand." Ironically, the economic concept of scarcity suggests a high "value" for serial-killers at the margin. By comparison, criminal psychologists and business-like murderers, for example, are relatively more plentiful. On the basis of scarcity, assuming that all other factors are held constant, this results in a lower marginal valuation. It is the difference in marginal valuations that explains why many criminal psychologists would love to advance their careers -- within the criminal justice system and in the eyes of the fascinated public -- through the apprehension of a highly valued serial-killer. (This is analogous to a reporter who seeks a "sensational story" in order to advance his or her career.) However, since there are many more business-like murderers, police investigators are more likely to be pointed in the wrong direction by self-interested criminal psychologists. This could be especially bad if criminal psychologists and/or profilers attempt to create "serial-killers" from witnesses in cases of business-like murder. (For a reporter this would be similar to embellishing an otherwise mundane piece of news.) Because of their motivation, criminal psychologists are more likely to end up as unwitting accomplices in many business-like murders.

Regardless of whether the offender's objectives are wealth or are psychologically or emotionally based, the offender's level of emotions and/or the degree of rational calculation prior to choosing the homicide alternative is a general indicator of whether a homicide should be considered as emotionally motivated (HR is false) or rationally motivated (HR is true). If a homicide is not committed rashly, such as on the basis of powerful emotions, then it is assumed that the offender has more time available for information processing and rational calculation prior to making his or her choice of alternatives. In other words, information should be near perfect and rationality should be relatively unbounded. The greater time resource allows the offender to increase the level of attained utility (that is, to choose more optimally) by considering and implementing, prior to the event, any and all methods that will reduce apprehension risk (p).

When wealth is sought, the methods used to reduce the risk of apprehension may include the use of more experienced offenders. Experienced offenders will have observed any and all law enforcement weaknesses and will have discussed which techniques work the best. Thus in the case of business-like homicides in which maximum wealth enhancement (that is, von Neuman-Morgenstern utility) is sought optimizing behavior should be expected to occur. The likelihood of optimizing behavior is reinforced by the fact that it is easier to imagine planning activities, especially if they involve professionals, being conducted rationally rather than under circumstances involving powerful emotions. Moreover, the involvement of experienced and, therefore, desensitized homicide offenders may further inhibit the role of powerful emotions. Experienced and desensitized homicide offenders can be assumed to be motivated on the basis of rationality. To put this another way, it does not appear reasonable to assume that hit-men would travel some distance, kill a particular individual at a particular place and time (and possibly stage the crime scene so that it appears to be other than a professional homicide), leave little or no evidence and then calmly drive away all strictly on the basis of emotion.

Even a homicide opportunity that simply falls into a wealth seeking offender's lap is more likely to be recognized as an opportunity by an experienced, rational offender. An experienced offender is already aware of how to murder someone such that the risk of apprehension (p) would be minimal. Extensive planning (as an expression of rational calculation) may, therefore, not always be associated with murder as a business decision. However, when apprehension does not occur and wealth gains (G) are realized, then rational calculation as the primary basis for homicidal action cannot be assumed away. In contrast, a less experienced offender is, by definition, less likely to consider homicide a wealth enhancing alternative.

The specific indicators or characteristics of emotionally motivated homicides appear to include inexperienced or first-time offenders who commit a homicide rashly for reasons other than wealth gains and without the coordinated efforts of other offenders. The increased likelihood of imperfect information and bounded rationality suggests that emotionally motivated offenders will tend to make suboptimal choices. The offender may have time to consider apprehension risk reducing actions (such as fleeing the crime scene or involving additional conspirators to remove or conceal evidence) only after the occurrence of the homicide event. Therefore, evidence that links the offender to the crime scene is more likely to be present. On the other hand, if sufficient time is available to the offender after the occurrence of the homicide, more extensive rational calculation is likely to manifest much less evidence. Also, predictable actions such as fleeing the crime scene may actually be more beneficial to the police in helping to identify the offender.

Offenders who are assumed to be motivated predominantly on the basis of rational calculation (and seek to obtain wealth related gains) are indicated by specific factors such other and more specialized offenders, more experienced offenders, planning, and wealth related objectives.

Limits to the application of economic analysis to the crime of murder appear to be related to not only the degree of rational calculation but also to the offender's level of information. The severe consequences of a homicide suggest that the level of information and, hence, level of rationality should be high. When rational calculation and information levels are significant a relatively complex decision model (such as SEU) appears to be appropriate. However, powerful emotions are expected to lead to urgency and rashness and, consequently, constrain the degree of rational calculation and information processing by decreasing decision making time. For emotionally motivated homicides (in which homicide is a choice among alternatives that might relieve powerful emotions) economic analysis is still appropriate but it may involve the use of decision models that can account for bounded rationality (or "satisficing" behavior) and suboptimal outcomes. One should also be aware that there are factors other than powerful emotions that can inhibit an offender's ability to acquire and/or process information. For example, an offender can be too young and/or mentally immature to fully understand the consequences of a homicide. Also, an offender may have a severe communication disorder that prevents the offender from fully understanding or being aware of homicide consequences. In the case of an offender who fears for his or her life a severe communication disorder may even make alternatives other than homicide irrational or, equivalently, irrelevant. From the typical person's point of view, homicides committed by offenders with information processing limitations may often appear   irrational and economic analysis may be inappropriate.[15]

Table 6.1 lists all of the non-negligent homicide circumstance categories in the supplemental homicide report (SHR) data. An SHR circumstance category is re-classified by referring to factors that indicate the predominance of either rational or emotional motivation in a circumstance category. In a given circumstance category, only those motive indicators that are reasonably expected to be the most frequent are included.

Table 6.1
Non-negligent Homicide Circumstances and Motivation

SHR Circumstance	Specific Motive Indicators	More Rational	More Emotional
Lover's triangle	Urgency, Rashness, Inexperience, Lone Acting, Non-wealth seeking		X
Child killed by baby-sitter	Rashness, Inexperience, Lone acting, Non-wealth Seeking, Unplanned		X
Brawls (due to influence of alcohol or narcotics)	Rashness, Unplanned, Non-wealth seeking		X
Argument over money[a]	Urgency, Rashness, Lone acting, Unplanned, Wealth	X	X
Other arguments	Urgency, Rashness, Lone acting, Unplanned		X
Gangland killing	Coordinated group, Experience, Planning, Wealth seeking (Criminal enterprise)	X	
Youth gang killing	Coordinated group, Experience, Planning, Wealth seeking (Territory or criminal enterprise)	X	
Institutional killings	Experience	X	
Sniper attacks[b]	Lone acting, Planning	X	X
Felony homicide[c]	Experience, Planning	X	

[a]Argument over money is classified as emotionally motivated in the statistical analysis.
[b]Sniper attacks are classified as rationally motivated.
[c]Felony Homicide includes all homicides committed during the commission of other felonies such as rape, robbery, arson, or relating to narcotics and drug laws, etc.

In table 6.1, "Argument Over Money" and "Sniper Attacks" are the only SHR circumstance categories that can not be clearly classified according to the general nature of the motive. It is assumed that any argument is itself emotionally motivated. Thus "Argument Over Money" as a homicide circumstance category can reasonably be classified as emotionally motivated. For "Sniper Attacks," lone acting offenders indicate the greater likelihood of emotional motivation while planning indicates that rational calculation may be the predominant motivation for choosing the homicide alternative. It is also not reasonable to assume that other motive indicators are consistently present. Since planning is likely to be a consistent specific motive indicator for "sniper attacks" and planning abates rashness or impulsiveness and, therefore, offsets or decreases the likelihood of powerful emotions, rational motivation is simply assumed.

In the categories "Institutional Killings" and "Felony Homicide" there may be a large proportion of circumstances in which the offender is motivated to kill more on the basis of frustration, fear or other emotions. A robbery or other felony might not go as planned, for example, and the offender then kills out of frustration. On the other hand, many apparently emotionally motivated homicides, including some institutional killings and felony homicides, may actually be rationally motivated and planned. An example would be an offender who intends to create a situation in which he or she must kill. On the basis of a reasonable first approximation and that experience and/or planning may frequently be involved it is only assumed that "institutional killings" and "felony homicide" tend to fit relatively more into the rationally motivated category.

The category "Lover's Triangle" is assumed to include only a smaller subset of offenses that involve a conspiracy to commit murder in which wealth gains are an objective. Without specific motive indicators the overall circumstance category of "lover's Triangle" can only be assumed to fall relatively more into the emotionally motivated category.

Determining the most appropriate, although somewhat subjective, taxonomy allows for all homicide circumstance categories, and all the data, to be used. On the other hand, omitting the two categories "institutional killings" and "felony homicide" may increase the statistical significance of the estimates.

Using table 6.1, (HRij) is designated as false (HRij = 0) for all non-negligent SHR circumstances in which the offender is classified as tending to be emotionally motivated. Homicide (HRij) is designated as true (HR = 1) for all other categories presumed to be primarily rationally motivated. In the 1983 SHR data this results in thirty-six percent of the observations being classified as rationally motivated and sixty-four percent being classified as emotionally motivated.

Decision Parameter Variables

The decision parameter vectors in the model to be estimated are (p_{ij}), (f_{ij}), (G_i), and (Y_j). Because risk reducing actions are consistent with maximizing von Neumann-Morgenstern utility (or, equivalently, the expected monetary value of wealth gains), the apprehension risk vector (p_{ij}) is probably the most important of the four decision parameter vectors. The importance of (p_{ij}) can be seen clearly from equation (6.1) where $EU_{hj} = p_j U_j (G_j - f_j) + (1-p_j)U_j (G_j)$. As apprehension risk (p_{ij}) approaches zero, EU_{hj} approaches the measured value of $U_j (G_j)$. Similarly, equation (6.3) indicates that apprehension risk reduction may result in expected gains that exceed the opportunity cost of a legitimate alternative so that $H_j = H_j (EU_{hj} - EU_{lj}) > 0$. This is especially likely for the risk-seeking offender. A zero value of apprehension risk (p_{ij}) means that $EU = G$ and that this value is marginally increasing. Clearly, the rationally motivated offender's assessment of the level of apprehension risk (p_{ij}) will be critical to the homicide decision.

The SHR data provide some easily observable factors that are expected to be related to offender (j's) assessment of the level of apprehension risk (p_{ij}) in homicide incident (i). These factors include the offender's sex (MLO), the jurisdictional population (JP) in which the incident occurs, the existence of a victim and offender relationship (VOR), the use of a gun (GUN) or knife (KNI), the total number of offenders (NOF) involved, and whether the homicide remains unsolved (UNS).[16]

In general, reducing apprehension risk (p) requires extensive information processing and rational calculation (or, equivalently, experience) on the part of the offender or offenders. Thus rationally motivated offenders may engage in more extensive planning and/or rely on the help of specialists. Planning may help determine the nature of crime scene staging, for example. The use of more experienced offenders may significantly reduce the chances of leaving "connecting evidence" at the crime scene. Together, extensive planning and the use of more experienced and specialized offenders may create an alibi. It seems less likely that these types of coordinated, purposeful multiple offender actions would be the norm in cases where a homicide is committed rashly and on the basis of powerful emotions. Therefore, multiple offenders (NOF) are expected to indicate a decrease in apprehension risk (p) and be directly related to rationally motivated homicides (HR).

Of course it is also possible that in some cases multiple offenders (NOF) will be associated with apparently spontaneous gang activities in which some gang members become involved in a homicide. In many such incidences, however, gang leaders may actually be manipulating subordinate gang members. Thus even in cases where multiple homicide offenders appear to simply be "followers" homicidal actions may actually be coordinated, purposeful and, therefore, appropriately related to (HR).

Unsolved homicides (UNS) directly indicate decreased apprehension risk (p). Therefore, unsolved homicides (UNS) are expected to be directly related to rational homicides (HR).

Evidence that police investigators can use to "connect" an offender to a victim or a crime scene increases apprehension risk (p). Several easily observable "connecting evidence" factors that are directly related to the probability of homicide solutions have been identified.[17] These factors are the existence of a victim and offender relationship and the use of a gun or knife by the offender. Since most homicides are emotionally motivated, police investigators usually consider those individuals with a classifiable victim and offender relationship as possible suspects. This obviously increases the apprehension risk (p) for an offender that is in fact related to the victim. Regarding the use of a gun or a knife, ballistics tests, blood stain analysis, finger print analysis, weapon possession (or even a suddenly missing weapon) can provide the means by which a suspect can be "connected" to a crime scene or a homicide victim. The existence of a victim and offender relationship (VOR) and the use of a gun (GUN)or knife (KNI) are "connecting evidence" factors that indicate increased apprehension risk (p) and are, therefore, expected to be inversely related to (HR).

On the average, the jurisdictional population of the police unit will be directly related to population density. Population density is, in turn, directly related to the risk of a witness being present. Also, homicide offenders may expect that larger police jurisdictions will tend to have more experienced homicide investigators. Thus a police unit's jurisdictional population is an easily observable factor that indicates a relatively higher level of apprehension risk from two possible sources (p). On the average then, the jurisdictional population (JP) in which homicide incident (i) occurs should be inversely related to (HR).

The percentage of all non-negligent homicides committed by males in the 1983 SHR data is sixty-three percent. That males are capable of greater levels of violent behavior than females may provide a partial explanation for the higher percentage of male offenders. However, it may also be true that preferences for risky choices are more prevalent among male offenders than among female offenders. A greater preference for risky choices would suggest that male offenders are also likely to be more sensitive to changes in the perceived level of apprehension risk (p). If males tend to prefer risky choices such as rationally motivated homicides and are, therefore, likely to be more sensitive to apprehension risk (p), then male offenders (MLO) will tend to indicate a decrease in apprehension risk (p) and be positively related to rationally motivated homicides (HR).

Easily observable factors that offender (j) can use to determine the expected level of punishment (f) in homicide event (i) are more difficult to find in the SHR data set. There is some evidence, although not conclusive, that black offenders who kill white victims are more likely to receive the death penalty than blacks who kill blacks.[18] However, it has also been pointed out that differences in punishment in such cases appear to be based on relevant factors such as excessive violence.[19] For these reasons, a homicide event (i) that involves a nonwhite offender (j) and a white victim may be directly related to the expected level of punishment (f). Since (f) is hypothesized to be inversely related to an assumed rationally motivated homicide (HR), the combination of a white victim-nonwhite offender (WVN) is expected to also be inversely related to (HR).

The SHR data provide two easily observable factors that are related to offender (j's) ability to assess wealth gains (G) in homicide event (i). These are the victim's age and the victim's race. In general, a victim's age is expected to be positively related to wealth gains (G) and the victim's status as non-white is expected to be, on the average, negatively related to (G). Since (G) is expected to be directly related to an assumed rationally motivated homicide (HR) the victim's age (VA) will also be directly related to (HR). Non-white victims (VNW) will be inversely related to (G) and, hence, to (HR).

Wealth gains from a legitimate alternative (Y) should be directly related to the offender (j's) level of human capital development. The SHR data provide two easily observable variables, offender (j's) age and race, that are related to human capital development. Offender (j's) age should be positively correlated with human capital development and to (Y). On the other hand, a nonwhite offender (j) is more likely to be correlated with fewer resources and lower human capital development and, therefore, to be inversely related to (Y). Since the wealth gains from legitimate alternative (Y) are expected to be inversely related to assumed rationally motivated homicide (HR), offender (j's) age (OA) should also be inversely related to (HR). Offender (j's) status as nonwhite (ONW) is expected to be inversely related to (Y) and directly related to (HR).

It is important to note that if the variables in the decision parameter vectors (G) and (Y) are statistically significant, then it can be inferred that wealth related gains are among those that are generally preferred by homicide offenders who are assumed to be rationally motivated. Moreover, statistical significance for vectors

(G) and (Y) would also imply that the set of assumed rationally motivated homicides (HR) substantially represent murder as a business decision.

Substituting the twelve SHR variables into the four decision parameter vectors (p_{ij}), (f_{ij}), (G_i) and (Y_j), results in equation (6.7) and the model to be estimated.

$$HR_{ij} = HR(MLO_{ij}, JP_{ij}, VOR_{ij}, GUN_{ij}, KNI_{ij}, NOF_{ij},$$
$$UNS_{ij}, WVN_{ij}, VA_i, VNW_i, OA_j, ONW_j). \qquad (6.7)$$

Brief definitions for each of the variables in equation (6.7) are as follows.

Dependent variable:

HR_{ij}: A rationally motivated and non-negligent homicide. HR_{ij} = 1 if yes and 0 otherwise.

Apprehension risk vector (p):

MLO_{ij}: The offender is male. MLO_{ij} = 1 if yes and 0 otherwise.

JP_{ij}: The population of the jurisdiction in which the incident occurred.

VOR_{ij}: There is a victim and offender relationship. VOR categories in the SHR data include husband, wife, common-law husband, common-law wife, mother, father, son, daughter, brother, sister, in-law, stepfather, stepmother, stepson, stepdaughter, other family, neighbor, acquaintance, boyfriend, girlfriend, ex-husband, ex-wife, employee, employer, friend, homosexual relationship, and other known relationship. VOR_{ij} = 1 if yes and 0 otherwise.

GUN_{ij}: The murder weapon is a gun. The SHR data define gun to include any type of firearm, handgun, rifle, shotgun, or other gun. GUN_{ij} = 1 if yes and 0 otherwise.

KNI$_{ij}$: The murder weapon is a knife. The SHR data define knife to include an ax, ice-pick, screwdriver, or any cutting instrument. KNI$_{ij}$ = 1 if yes and 0 otherwise.

NOF$_{ij}$: The number of offenders involved in the incident. (There is one incident record for each offender in the offender file. This provides individual characteristics for all offenders. On the other hand, it might also bias upwards the importance of NOF. This bias should be negligible, however, because multiple offenders occur in only four percent of the incidents.)

UNS$_{ij}$: The incident is report as unsolved in the monthly SHRs. UNS$_{ij}$ = 1 if yes and 0 otherwise.

Punishment vector (f):

WVN$_{ij}$: The victim is white and the offender is nonwhite. WVN$_{ij}$ = 1 if yes and 0 otherwise.

Wealth gains vector (G):

VA$_i$:   The victim's age in years.

VNW$_i$: The victim is nonwhite. VNW$_i$ = 1 if yes and 0 otherwise.

Legitimate alternative vector (Y):

OA$_j$:   The offender's age in years.

ONW$_j$: The offender is non-white. ONW$_{ij}$ = 1 if yes and 0 otherwise.

By including unsolved homicides (UNS) in the model some of the data for offenders will be missing. Missing data for an explanatory variable that is stochastic (random) can be replaced by its mean value (modal value for a discrete variable) calculated from the existing observations. This results in a zero order regression method in which the beta (β) estimates are nonbiased but no more efficient than estimates based on complete data.

The twelve variables that make up the four decision parameter vectors are easily observed characteristics that are specifically related to offender (j) and homicide event (i). Accordingly, these twelve variables also represent the hypothesized characteristics or profile of a homicide that is assumed to be rationally motivated. Moreover, the statistical significance of the variables in vectors (G) and (Y) will mean that these twelve variables also represent the hypothesized characteristics or profile of murder as a business decision.

Although equation (6.7) is the one estimated, the twelve variables actually represent only the four decision parameter vectors (p), (f), (Y), and (G). Therefore, any statistically significant variables serve only to support or refute the more general model represented by equation (6.5). If the model is specified correctly and in accordance with economic theory, the significance of the four decision parameters will support the inference that homicide offenders who commit homicides that are defined or assumed to be rationally motivated are, in fact, behaving as if they were rational.

EMPIRICAL RESULTS AND PROFILE

Since the dependent variable (HR) in equation (6.7) is discrete, equation (6.7) is a qualitative response model and is estimated using a maximum likelihood logit procedure. Table 6.2 presents the results. Notice that the attained significance indicated by the log likelihood chi-squared statistic in table 6.2 is very high. Any loss in efficiency due to missing offender data in unsolved cases (UNS) and the zero order regression method does not appear to be very significant. This indicates that the model explains rationally motivated homicides (HR) very well. The hypothesized profile characteristics appear to be generally consistent with predictions. The direction of effect for all explanatory variables is as expected and the only statistically insignificant variables are WVN and MLO. The statistical significance of all variables in the (G) and (Y) vectors indicate that equation (6.7) is essentially a model of murder as a business decision.

Table 6.2
Rationally Motivated Homicide Characteristics

VARIABLE	ESTIMATE	T-RATIO	WALD CHI-SQUARE
INTERCEPT	-0.0239	-0.2673	0.0717
MLO	0.0439	0.8459	0.7157
JP	-0.0000000097	-11.8987	150.4050**
VOR	-0.5680	-14.6392	214.0492**
GUN	-0.6380	-16.5714	275.0452**
KNI	-0.9116	-19.1916	367.5881**
NOF	0.4961	23.1822	537.1011**
UNS	0.5911	6.3152	39.8483**
WVN	-0.0682	-0.6380	0.4069
VA	0.0021	2.4970	6.2079
VNW	-0.5765	-5.9927	35.8745**
OA	-0.0113	-11.0784	123.5132**
ONW	0.5364	5.5528	30.8468**

Note: Maximum Likelihood Logit Results with n = 21,128. The log likelihood ratio chi-square test statistic is 2116.126 (12 d.f.). At a .01 level of significance the critical value is 26.217.
* At a .05 level of significance the critical value is 3.841.
** At a .01 level of significance the critical value is 6.635.

Since the variable white victim-nonwhite offender (WVN) is assumed to represent an offender's assessment of the level of punishment (f), consideration of increased punishment does not appear to be a statistically significant influence on the decision to commit a rationally motivated homicide. The relative insignificance of punishment (f) is consistent with the implication that rationally motivated offenders are expected to be more sensitive to different levels of apprehension risk (p). On the other hand, it is also possible that WVN is not widely held to lead to relatively greater levels of punishment. Thus there may be a problem with using

WVN to represent the decision parameter vector (f). The statistical insignificance of male offenders (MLO) in the risk vector (p) suggests that a preference for risky choices among rationally motivated homicide offenders is not a predominantly male characteristic and/or that male offenders are not more sensitive to apprehension risk than female offenders.

The probability that each individual homicide is rationally motivated is calculated from the logit results. Table 6.3 presents the average values of each of the statistically significant variables in table 6.2 in terms of increasing probabilities of rational motivation. Notice, for example, how the jurisdictional population (witness and/or experienced investigator risk) decreases in value and the number of offenders (organizational specialization) increases as the probability of (HR) increases.

Table 6.3
Statistically Significant Emotional or Rational Homicide Characteristics

Vector/ Variable	Average Value	High Emotional Motivation ←———————————————→ High Rational Motivation			
		P(HR≤.25)	P(HR≤.50)	P(HR≥.50)	P(HR≥.75)
Number of Observations	21,128	5,760	17,648	3,480	439
p JP	1,368,262	1,872,221	1,351,788	730,042	477,625
VOR	.541	.831	.602	.235	.308
GUN	.590	.552	.639	.341	.244
KNI	.214	.439	.242	.071	.144
NOF	1.320	1.028	1.133	2.268	4.330
UNS	.243	.088	.234	.291	.005
G VA	34.992	34.588	33.931	40.373	41.221
VNW	.453	.617	.499	.216	.221
Y OA	49.688	47.941	50.180	47.196	23.989
ONW	.614	.577	.609	.644	.569

Note: Statistical Significance from table 1.

The logit coefficients in table 6.2 represent nonlinear relationships. Only the signs, or direction of effect, and statistically significance can be determined directly from the logit results. The marginal effect that each variable has on the probability of rational motivation cannot be directly determined. This problem can be remedied by OLS estimation using, from the logit results, the calculated probability that each observation is rationally motivated as the dependent variable. The calculated probabilities create a continuous dependent variable that is a linear combination of the dependent variables in equation (6.7). Thus the goodness of fit measures will appear exceptionally good. However, any biases in the data, such as with the possible over stated importance of NOF, will be amplified. OLS estimation provides the constant "on average" marginal percentage point effect for each variable on (HR) as well as standardized coefficients. The standardized coefficients allow each variable to be ranked in terms of its relative importance regardless of that variable's unit of measurement. The OLS results and variable ranking are provided in table 6.4.

Table 6.4
OLS Results and Standardized Coefficient Ranking

Variable and [Rank]	Percentage Point Effect	T-Ratio	Standardized Coefficient
Intercept	0.4950	986.697	0.0000
NOF [1]	0.1056	786.702	0.5545
KNI [2]	-0.2002	-617.121	-0.5431
OA [3]	-0.0022	-347.598	-0.4803
GUN [4]	-0.1455	-533.172	-0.4736
VOR [5]	-0.1237	-477.340	-0.4082
VNW [6]	-0.1146	-414.182	-0.3777
ONW [7]	0.1059	336.414	0.3413
UNS [8]	0.1027	194.807	0.2919
JP [9]	-1.9818E-8	-383.929	-0.2722
VA [10]	0.0005	82.321	0.0574

Note: Adjusted R^2 = 0.9902. The average value of the standardized coefficients in each of the three statistically significant vectors is p = 0.4239, Y = 0.4108, and G = 0.2176. WVN and MLO are omitted because they are not statistically significant in table 1. Also, the relative importance of NOF may be overstated.

The average values of the standardized coefficients associated with apprehension risk (p), legitimate wealth gains or opportunity cost (Y), and homicide wealth gains (G) are, respectively, 0.4239, 0.4108, and 0.2176. The variable WVN and, therefore, the punishment vector (f) is statistically insignificant. This clearly indicates the relative importance of the risk (p) vector.

The rationally motivated (or murder as a business decision) homicide profile characteristics are based on the variables contained in the statistically significant parameter vectors. These characteristics are grouped by the vector in which they belong and then listed below in order of the relative importance of each vector.

Apprehension Risk Vector (p)

1.   Planning and gains from organizational specialization are exemplified by multiple offenders per incident or (NOF). Table 6.4 indicates that, on the average, each offender involved in a given incident increases the probability that the incident is rationally motivated by about 11 percentage points.

2.   Deliberate attempts to reduce the availability of "connecting evidence" at the crime scene is indicated by (GUN) and (KNI) to be relatively important. This should not be misinterpreted to mean that a gun or knife would not be used. However, if they are used it is probably that they would be unlikely to be found.

3.   On the average, the lack of a classifiable victim and offender relationship (VOR) increases the probability that a homicide is rationally motivated by about 12 percentage points. Table 6.3 indicates that VOR occurs less than half as often in homicides with high probabilities of rational motivation. Alternatively stated, the lack of a VOR decreases the probability of an emotionally motivated homicide.[20]

4.   On the average, homicides reported as unsolved (UNS) at the end of any monthly reporting period have an increased probability of being rationally motivated of about 10 percentage points. UNS suggests better or near perfect information such as when experienced (older) offenders are involved. However, table 6.3 also indicates an average percentage point decrease in UNS that is

correlated with decreases in average offender age and increases in the number of offenders. Thus the level of experience and professionalism of the offenders can be inferred to be very important in homicide solutions.

5. Jurisdictional population (JP) indicates that rationally motivated homicide offenders will consider the risk of witness presence and deliberately attempt to reduce that risk. Because killing a witness is included in felony homicide as one of the categories that make up the dependent variable (HR), the measured effect of JP is a separate or independent effect. The inverse relationship between (JP) and (HR) may also indicate that rationally motivated homicide offenders consider investigator experience and effectiveness (and, hence, apprehension risk) to be inversely related to (JP). The relative importance of the risk of witness presence and investigator effectiveness effects cannot be determined.

Opportunity Cost Vector (Y)

1. Wealth related gains from the best legitimate alternative (Y) will be relatively low. This is indicated by offenders that tend to be younger (OA) and nonwhite (ONW). The relative importance of the (Y) vector and the statistical significance of OA are consistent with the suggestion by James Q. Wilson in that the legitimate alternative (Y) is more important to non-professional (younger) criminals.[21]

Gains Vector (G)

1. In the (G) vector, wealth related gains are indicated by older victims (VA) and a decreasing tendency for nonwhite victims (VNW). Thus rationally motivated homicides (HR) are characterized by wealth related preferences in both the (Y) and (G) decision parameter vectors. This is consistent with murder as a business decision.

PROFILE IMPLICATIONS

There are some implications of the profile for rationally motivated homicides that are related to deterrence production. For rationally motivated, business-like murders, the greatest deterrence payoff is likely to occur from resources that are directed toward increasing apprehension risk (p). This is because the apprehension risk vector (p) appears to be the most important. In contrast, the punishment vector (f) is indicated to be statistically insignificant. This suggests a very limited deterrence payoff from increased resources allocated there. Re-allocating societies' resources toward increasing (Y) will deter only a small fraction of the overall set of non-negligent homicide offenders. Specifically, table 6.3 indicates that policies aimed at increasing (Y) would only effect the 439 offenders (about two percent of the total of 21,128) in the most rational class of homicides where $P(HR \geq .75)$.

Regarding criminal investigations, the rationally motivated profile is not simply extrapolating past homicide experience in order to predict or hypothesize unknown offender characteristics. This profile focuses more on the characteristics of the crime "murder as a business decision" rather than individual offender characteristics. By definition, the wealth gains objective cannot change and it is unlikely that the means of achieving this objective will change. The statistical significance of the (Y) and (G) vectors suggest that a relatively straight forward cost-benefit analysis can help identify offenders that are rationally motivated. For example, if a homicide occurs that remains unsolved and that appears to be characterized as rationally motivated, the fact that measurable homicide gains are actually realized by someone would be an indicator of that person's guilt. For a given suspect, if the gains realized in (G) are, in fact, greater than those that could be realized in (Y) there is an even higher probability that the suspect is the actual offender (or is one of the actual offenders). The same logic applies to anyone who might potentially gain wealth (G) from the homicide. If, due perhaps to a previous criminal investigation of organized crime, the value of (Y) is negative, wealth gains

(G) may not actually be observed. The ability to objectively identify specific offenders based upon characteristics related to wealth gains that must, by definition, be relevant to this type of crime is a clear advantage over existing criminal profiles. This advantage and the fact that the rationally motivated criminal profile has very high statistical significance may enhance its potential for admissibility in court.

The motivation to action continuum that involves emotions and/or rational calculation appears to be generally relevant. Because the apprehension risk vector (p) is expected to be highly important to wealth maximizing offenders and relatively less important to emotionally motivated and/or less efficient offenders, the apprehension risk vector should highlight clearly the specific nature of the rational-emotional continuum. Figure 6.1 illustrates the rational-emotional continuum by taking each of the four (HR) probability categories from table 6.3 and the most important characteristics in the risk (p) vector: NOF, KNI, GUN, VOR, and UNS. The least important risk (p) vector characteristic, JP, is not included in figure 6.1 because of scaling problems. In each of the four (HR) probability categories the average values of the risk vector characteristics and a ratio consisting of the number of offenders in that category to total offenders in the sample are plotted in terms of the rational-emotional continuum. Figure 6.1 indicates that, except for unsolved (UNS), the probabilities of rational motivation greater than $P(HR \geq .50)$ are associated with a relatively significant and consistent divergence in the values of the apprehension risk related characteristics from their emotional motivation values. This divergence suggests that, on the average, homicides primarily motivated by unbounded rational calculation have characteristics that differ significantly from those associated with rationally bounded (emotional) motivation. The differences in these characteristics may assist criminal investigators in identifying murder as a business decision.

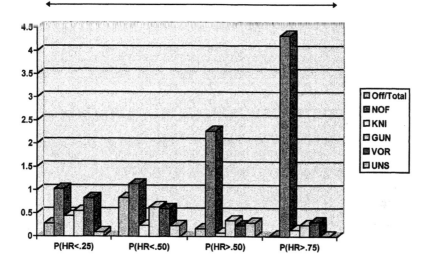

High Emotional Motivation
(Low Rational Motivation)
High Rational Motivation
(Low Emotional Motivation)

Fig. 6.1. Frequency Distribution for Emotional-Rational Characteristics in the Risk of Apprehension Vector. The variable JP is omitted.

It should be pointed out that distinguishing emotionally motivated from rationally motivated homicides is a first step in any homicide investigation. If possible, this task should precede any attempt to identify an offender or offenders through a cost benefit analysis.

The statistical results in table 6.3 provide another important implication to criminal investigation. This is that offender age (OA) and unsolved (UNS) both decrease significantly when $P(HR \geq .75)$. Figure 6.2 illustrates this graphically. In Figure 6.2 the values of (UNS) from table 6.3 have been multiplied by 100 to facilitate comparison with offender (OA). As an assumed reflection of human capital in the (Y) vector, (OA) is expected to be directly related to (Y) as a measure of the wealth related opportunity cost of legitimate alternatives. Offender age (OA) is therefore expected be, and is, inversely related to rationally motivated homicides (HR) in the logit results in table 6.2. However, offender age (OA) should also be directly related to the level of offender experience. Of course, if offender age (OA) is directly related to experience, then offender age (OA) should also be directly related to unsolved homicides (UNS). The expected direct relationship between (OA) and (UNS) is identified clearly only in table 6.3 and in figure 6.2. Obviously, the level of offender experience is important in solving murder as a business decision. The apprehension of inexperienced business-like homicide offenders should, therefore, be commonly expected news headlines. In contrast, highly experienced business-like homicide offenders (such as highly professional hit-men) are unlikely to be the subject of frequent news headlines.

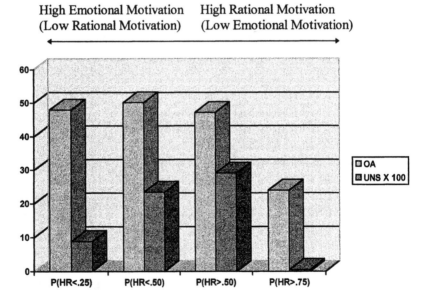

Fig. 6.2. Frequency Distribution for Offender Age (OA) and Unsolved Homicide (UNS x 100)

In summary, the profile for rationally motivated homicides appears to be applicable to approximately one-third of all non-negligent homicides that occurred in 1983. This is a much broader range of applicability than criminal profiles that are currently in use. The new and more broadly applicable criminal profile also rests on a solid theoretical (economic) foundation, is not biased such that it points away from rationally motivated offenders seeking wealth gains, has highly significant statistical support, and can help identify rationally motivated homicides as well as individual suspects. It appears that the profile for rationally motivated homicides may be able to achieve the objective of helping police investigators become more effective and efficient in solving the most common type of rationally motivated homicide: murder as a business decision.

SUGGESTED READINGS

1.   Marché, G. E. "The Production of Homicide Solutions: An Empirical Analysis," *The American Journal of Economics and Sociology* 53 (October 1994):385-401.

2.   Marché, G. E. "Mending a Hole in the Police Dragnet: A Criminal Profile for Rationally Motivated Homicides," *Forensics: The Electronic Journal of the American College of Forensic Examiners* , Spring 1996.

CHAPTER 7
CRIMINAL JUSTICE SYSTEM PRODUCTION

Deterrence in the form of negative incentives that increase the cost of crime is an important output produced by the criminal justice system. All else held constant, more criminal justice system resources and greater efficiency in their allocation and use are required to increase deterrence production and reduce the level of crime in our society. Allocation efficiency requires that increased levels of resources be applied to the most seriously deficient areas of criminal justice system production. One such area is the apparent "hole in the police dragnet" through which experienced and rationally motivated homicide offenders routinely pass. An increase in the use of specialized resources and increased training in economic theory appears likely to improve deterrence production in this area. This chapter also discusses production issues related to the risk of conviction and rehabilitation and incapacitation.

BAD POLICIES

There are good arguments made by well intentioned individuals against increasing deterrence in the form of negative incentives to crime. For example, on his July 23, 1996, television program Jerry Spence argued that politicians promising more police and police resources to combat crime are simply trying to get votes by saying something simple that people want to here. According to Jerry Spence, these politicians are simply trading votes for our kids! Spence argues that children born to single mothers on welfare (who are often presumed to also be drug addicts) have only committed the crime of being born to the wrong mother. These presumably neglected kids then grow up and join street gangs out of the need for survival. Spence also implies that children born to more functional and carrying parents will not go on to commit crimes. According to Spence, increasing deterrence against crime through increased police presence would be analogous to poring gasoline on an already raging fire. Spence's alternative solution to the juvenile crime problem is to temporarily adopt these kids out of their environment and into the homes of caring individuals. These carrying individuals could then show these kids that there are other ways of doing things. Jerry Spence's argument certainly sounds appealing! Unfortunately, it is also very misguided and naive.

The real world works more like the following true story. Some friends of ours succeeded in being awarded the custody of their sixteen-year-old juvenile nephew who was facing jail-time for crimes committed in another State. The juvenile court made it very clear to the nephew that if he ever ran away from his aunt and uncle he would be sent directly to jail. The juvenile nephew was raised in a dysfunctional family in which the presence of illegal drugs and fighting was the norm. His mother was married to a person other than the juvenile nephew's father. The juvenile nephew was a member of the street gang known as the CRIPS. The nephew stated that he had run away from countless (20 or more) foster homes. When asked why he had run away so many times the nephew would always laugh and say it was because he never got into trouble from doing so. This is true. Congress enacted the Juvenile Justice and Delinquency Prevention Act (JJDP) in 1974. The JJDP Act's central mandate requires States to remove all status offenders from juvenile detention and correctional facilities. Status offenders are youth, such as runaways and truants, who have committed offenses that would not be crimes if they had been committed by adults.

The nephew also stated several times that he would not work for the minimum wage because he could make much more money dealing drugs and engaging in other illegal activities. As it happens, the nephew's real father was an active member of a motorcycle gang in a different State. He was also a known drug dealer with outstanding police warrants for his arrest. Interestingly, the nephew reported that his father had the means to take a vacation in the Bahamas every year!

The aunt and uncle taking custody of their juvenile nephew were caring, well adjusted, mature adults. The aunt was a highly experienced speech pathologist who was familiar with the psychology of juveniles and with behavior modification techniques. After living with his aunt and uncle for about six months, the nephew ran away. He is then suspected to have, with the aid of friends, burglarized his aunt and uncle's house. Over $1,500.00 worth of property was stolen. The juvenile nephew was held in custody on the burglary charge for a few days but was scheduled for release because it was only his first offense in his new State of residence. His aunt and uncle took custody of their nephew and drove him back to his home State where he was then sent to jail. According to the authorities in the his home State, the six months that the nephew lived with his aunt and uncle was the longest time that he had ever remained out of trouble.

Social workers had warned the aunt and uncle that because he was raised in an unstable and violent household the nephew would prefer exciting activities. The social worker's admonition is clearly consistent with the economic assumption of constant preferences. The aunt and uncle made every attempt to accommodate the nephew's preferences for exciting activities by playing pool, tennis, and football with their nephew. They also allowed their nephew his normal ration of beer and cigarettes--and even allowed him to play rap music on their car radio. All of these things were consistent with his previous consumption patterns and stated preferences. Unfortunately, their nephew's preferences for committing crimes, running away, and living with other similar juveniles had not diminished. Although economists have not tried to explain or account for preferences in the past, Gary Becker's new book ACCOUNTING FOR TASTES,[1] indicates that preferences are consistent because of past experiences, including those in childhood, behavioral habits, and because of peer effects. A person's attitudes (such as toward risk) and beliefs also explain preferences. Peer effects appeared to play a very significant role in the tastes and preferences of the juvenile nephew.

Unlike some would indicate, many legitimate income producing opportunities for juveniles are usually available. Unfortunately, legitimate alternatives tend to involve hard work. Not surprisingly, the juvenile nephew repeatedly indicated (using different terminology, of course) that legitimate income producing alternatives were only a relatively insignificant opportunity cost to criminal activities. From the juvenile nephew's point of view, why should anyone want to suffer the mundane consequences of washing dishes, sweeping floors, handling inventory, or doing homework? The negative consequences of illegal drug selling (or, in the nephew's case burglarizing his aunt and uncle's house) involved only the minor inconvenience of arrest. The inconvenience of arrest is more than offset by the money received from drug selling (or burglary) and the positive consequences of arrest.[2] In the case of the juvenile nephew, there was little or no inconvenience associated with arrest. Instead, there were positive consequences of arrest on the burglary charge that included free food, temporary shelter, television, games, a quick release, and an increased status among peers. With only positive incentives to crime provided by the criminal justice system it is clearly rational for juveniles to sell illegal drugs and commit crimes!

Going back to Jerry Spence's solution to the juvenile crime problem, it appears more likely that adopting a juvenile gang member into a more normal household would be like inviting part of a raging forest fire into your house and then expecting the fire to suddenly prefer not to burn! In the case of the juvenile nephew who stayed out of trouble for six months it was clear that consistent preferences simply kept the fire smoldering until the right opportunity came along. Perhaps it is better to pour some water on the fire instead. Water has the effect of reducing the opportunity for the fire to burn. By analogy, pouring water on the crime fire involves increasing police presence (the risk of apprehension) and the level of punishment. This decreases the opportunity (by increasing costs) to commit crimes. Unfortunately, the crime fire has been invited into our society and encouraged to burn out of control by policies such as the Juvenile Justice and Delinquency Prevention Act of 1974.

THE NEED FOR MORE CJS RESOURCES

In addition to bad policies that contribute to criminal behavior, it appears that there may either be too few resources aimed at producing deterrence and/or that existing criminal justice system are producing deterrence vary inefficiently. Table 7.1, presents some indicators for homicide and all index crimes for 1960 and 1991 that clearly indicate that the probability and severity of punishment for homicide and all index crimes have generally been falling over the last three decades. All else held constant, higher homicide and crime rates are the predicted result.

Table 7.1
Crime and Law Enforcement Indicators for Homicide and Index Crimes[a], 1960 and 1991

	Crime Rate (Per 100,000)		Median (Mean) Time Served in State Prisons in Months		Percentage of Offenses Known to Police Cleared by Arrest		[c]Probability of Imprisonment (State Prisons)	
	1960	1991	1960	1991	1960	1991	1960	1991
Murder and Non-Negligent Man-slaughter	5.1	9.8	52.0[b] (121.4)	68.0 (84.0)	92.3	67.2	39.8[d]	28.4
All Index Crimes	1887.2	5897.3	NA (28.4)	17.1 (24.1)	30.8	21.3	2.8	0.8

Source: Data from Issac Ehrlich, "Crime, Punishment, and the Market for Offenses," *Journal of Economic Perspectives*, v10, n1 (Winter, 1996) p 45.

[a] Index crimes include murder and non-negligent manslaughter, forcible rape, robbery, aggravated assault, burglary, larceny, and auto theft.
[b] 1960 median time is for homicide, including negligent manslaughter.
[c] Percentage of those entering state prisons relative to offenses known.
[d] 1960 probability is for homicide, including negligent manslaughter.

If deterrence is a good and the level of public sector homicide or crime deterrence production is insufficient to meet the level of deterrence demanded, then private sector deterrence production should be expected to occur as a means of meeting the level demanded. The need for additional private sector deterrence production can be seen by referring to figure 7.1.

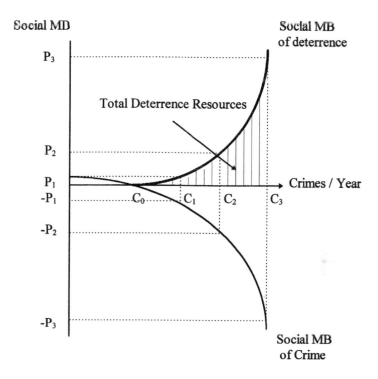

Fig. 7.1. Involuntary Consumption of Crime. Like too much snow or mud, the marginal benefit of crime will eventually become negative such as at $-P_1$, $-P_2$, and $-P_3$ as the level of crime increases. At the margin, society is willing to pay prices such as P_1, P_2, and P_3 to deter crime. The total amount of resources society is willing to devote to crime deterrence is given by the positive area under the marginal benefit of deterrence curve. If resources (taxes) paid for public sector deterrence reduce crime from C_3 to C_2, then all crime between C_2 and C_0 is subject to being deterred privately.

In figure 7.1 a number of crimes occur during a year and must be "consumed" by citizens involuntarily or against their wishes. In other words, crime is not a "good" but is a negative externality like air, noise, or water pollution. However, for small amounts of crime, the marginal utility (benefit) of crime could be positive. This might be the case if small levels of crime are associated with increased individual freedoms and more exciting activities. This would also hold true for moderate amounts of rain, snow or mud. In this sense, there is a demand or positive marginal benefit for crime or rain, snow and mud. Beyond some point, however, too much crime, like too much rain, snow or mud, must ultimately result in increasingly negative marginal benefits. The negative value of crime at the margin is given by prices $-P_1$, $-P_2$, and $-P_3$ that correspond to crime levels C_1, C_2, and C_3, respectively.

A negative marginal value for something that is no longer a "good" represents the maximum amount that society will pay to get rid of the last unit of it (e.g., water, snow or mud) or, similarly, to deter the last unit of crime. In other words, efficiently removing or deterring something with a negative value generates a positive marginal value or benefit that must at least offset the negative marginal value of the existing "bad." Once the "bad" is gone or deterred, the marginal value should be at least zero.

In figure 7.1 the positive values P_1, P_2, and P_3 represent the corresponding maximum value of deterring an incremental unit of crime and the shaded area under the positive value curve and above the horizontal axis represents the maximum amount of resources that society would be willing to devote to crime deterrence. A portion of those resources (as taxes) paid to public sector law enforcement may reduce crime from C_3 to C_2, for example. However, if public sector deterrence production was more efficient then the same amount of taxes might deter all crimes between C_3 and C_1. In the absence of greater efficiency or more taxes paid to law enforcement, all crime between C_2 and C_0 must be deterred by private sector production. Private expenditures on things such as better locks, guard dogs, and the employment of private security guards, for example, produce additional crime deterrence. However, if the level of crime still remains so high that people begin to fear for their lives then it is reasonable to expect them to want to take more extreme and costly measures to deter crime. For example, some citizens may be willing to assume the responsibility for and incur the cost and inconvenience of carrying a firearm in order to deter an assault. Younger citizens may also be compelled to carry weapons and to join armed gangs as a means of assuring their personal security. In essence, the failure to increase public sector deterrence to adequate levels, either through greater efficiency or more resources, may result not only in more crime but also the increasing armament of the citizenry.[3]

Targeting Resources to Maximize Returns

If the objective is to reduce crime rates, it is essential that more deterrence be produced by the criminal justice system. Adding more resources to deterrence producing units of the criminal justice system should directly increase the risks of apprehension, conviction, and punishment and increase the level of punishment for most crimes. There would, however, still be areas of weakness and inefficiency that need to be specifically targeted. One such area involves murder as a business decision. As previously indicated, existing theories of crime and criminal behavior do not adequately address murder as a business decision. It is probably also true that many professional scholars, some of who may even be involved in training police officers, do not even believe that such a crime exists! Attitudes and beliefs about crime and criminal behavior that are combined with a lack of training in rationally motivated crimes such as murder as a business decision suggests that specific improvements are needed in this area. Regarding such specifics, an empirical study by the author indicates that eight factors associated with the availability of evidence, community preferences for solutions, investigator experience, and investigator workload are indicated to have a statistically significant effect on the probability of homicide solutions.[4] The eight factors and there associated "on average" percentage point contributions to the probability of a homicide solution are ranked in order of their importance. The Factors that most decrease the probabilities of homicide solutions are the lack of a classifiable victim and offender relationship (minus 48 percentage points) and rationally motivated homicides (minus 17 percentage points). These two factors are also common characteristics of murder as a business decision. When compared to the much more common emotionally motivated homicides (that also typically have victim and offender relationships) business-like homicides have, on the average, a 65 percentage point decrease in solution probability. Empirical evidence such as this clearly indicates a hole in the police dragnet for murder as a business decision.

It should be pointed out that the author's study referred to above does not provide a way to determine whether the negative effect of rational motivation on homicide solutions is due more to criminal productivity or to the lack of police productivity (or any of its specific causes). Thus it may very well be that rationally motivated homicides could be investigated more effectively if police received training in economic reasoning. Unfortunately, training of this type is not ordinarily required or readily available. It appears reasonable to suggest that criminal justice system resources be allocated toward improving the effectiveness and efficiency of police investigations in the area of rationally motivated homicides or, equivalently, murder as a business decision.

The Vince Foster Case

It is useful to provide an actual case that highlights the possible consequences of failing to train police investigators to recognize murder as a business decision.[5] Vincent W. Foster, Jr., deputy White House counsel and close friend of President Clinton and former law partner Hillary Rodham Clinton, was found dead on July 20, 1993. Foster was the Clinton's attorney on their Whitewater real estate investment. After a cursory investigation by the U. S. Park Police and some of the investigators working for special counsel Robert B. Fisk, Jr., the government closed the case as an apparent suicide. Fisk's report indicated that Foster died of a self-inflicted gunshot wound at Fort Marcy Park in Virginia, the location where his body was found.

The Foster case may very well be one in which improperly trained, careless, and inexperienced investigators have been easily fooled by more experienced and/or professional homicide offenders. A much more thorough investigation by Vincent J. Scalice, funded by the Western Journalism Center and prepared by Scalice and Santucci of Forensic Control systems, Inc., finds numerous inconsistencies in the Fisk report. The investigative report concludes that "homicide has not been ruled out . . . person's unknown may have obstructed justice in the death of one of the highest ranking officials to die under suspicious circumstances since the death of President Kennedy." The results of this report are based on a crime scene reconstruction at Fort Marcy Park, on autopsy reports and testimony given by individuals present at the crime scene, and on forensic evidence and a detailed analysis of the FBI lab reports. Evidence was found that supports the following inconsistencies with the alleged suicide:

1. There were inconsistencies between FBI lab tests and evidence from a crime scene reconstruction.
   a. Although Foster is alleged to have walked more than 700 feet to the site where he was found, no soil was found on his clothing and shoes in FBI lab tests.
   b. On the path Foster was said to have been found clothing and three pairs of shoes worn by a model had soil on them.
   c. There were also grass stains on the soles of the shoes worn by the model but the FBI report does not mention any such stains.
2. There were inconsistencies between a normal suicide and the way Foster was found.
   a. Experts determined that the gun explosion should have propelled Foster's arms to his sides and at an angle to the body. Instead, Foster's body was found neatly arranged with his arms at his sides.
   b. In contrast to the orderly positioning of the body, Foster's eyeglasses were found approximately 13 feet from the body. Experts concluded that the eyeglasses could not have gotten that far from the body by natural means.
   c. Gunpowder residues indicated that neither Foster's left nor right hand was on the hand grip when it was fired. Moreover, the orderly positioning of the gun in Foster's hand indicates a high probability that the gun was staged in the hand.
3. There was an indication that the body may have been moved.
   a. After his alleged suicide, an FBI analysis of blood tracks on Foster's face indicted that his head was in as many as four different positions.
   b. Although the bullet exited the top rear of the head there was no blood splatter or other tissue in that location. Medical examiner

testimony indicates that blood had matted or congealed on the back of Foster's head indicating that the wound may have been covered if the body was moved.

c.   Foster's body was covered with carpet fibers of various colors.

Although it is possible that Vince Foster may have actually committed suicide, the crime scene was tampered with and obstruction of justice clearly occurred. A crime scene that is so extensively tampered with and that truly involves a suicide is inconsistent with reason. Why, for example, would anyone want to make a suicide look more like a homicide? Also, if Foster actually committed suicide somewhere else and his body was subsequently moved, what would be the net benefits gained? The benefits would have to be at least as great as the costs of obviously obstructing justice and becoming a homicide suspect. It is hard to imagine that Foster committed suicide in any place that would justify moving the body and incurring such great costs.

Only politically motivated individuals would attempt to explain away the Vince Foster case as something that is not suspicious. Moreover, guilty individuals would surely be among those who would be the happiest to see this case quietly swept under the washboards. It has been reported that there is evidence (hairs found on Foster's clothing) that tie at least one such individual to the crime scene. Circumstantial evidence such as this can not be lied about or avoided. Instead, such evidence represents, as TV's Lt. Columbo was found of saying, "some loose ends that need to be tied-up" (no pun intended). If there is a conspiracy (to commit murder) involved in this case it is clearly not one that emanates from the right wing. Protecting a suspect or suspects from investigation through political means (i.e., a guaranteed Presidential pardon) represents not only a decrease in risk (and, thereby, an explanation for the occurrence of such a crime), it represents a further obstruction of justice.

The bottom line appears to be that the findings in the Scalice and Santucci report support, at the very least, obstruction of justice in the case of Vince Foster's alleged suicide. Because Vince Foster's body appears to have been moved and the crime scene was staged there is also an indication that multiple homicide offenders may be involved. The possibility of multiple homicide offenders and crime scene staging suggest that the profile for rationally motivated homicides (or murder as a business decision) may be relevant. According to this profile, any individuals who actually realized, or who could have realized, wealth gains (including those that are political) from Foster's murder, especially if they could not have been gained by an alternative means, should be considered as suspects in the possible homicide of Vincent Foster.

Specialized Resources and Training

At the present time it is very unlikely that a murder committed by experienced, professional homicide offenders in which the motive is wealth (or is related such as with political gains) would be recognized as a business-decision murder by inexperienced investigators. Experienced and professional homicide offenders are likely to stage the crime scene so that a business-like murder will appear to be a different type of crime (such as a suicide) or even a different type of homicide. In addition to removing or destroying evidence, it would be very effective if, for example, the crime scene is staged to indicate a robbery and murder and/or bizarre behavior and psychopathology. A local and inexperienced police unit that seeks outside assistance in the investigation of such a homicide would probably end up requesting a criminal profile from the FBI. Not only would the criminal profile reduce the probability that the actual offenders would be apprehended, it would also magnify the social cost of the crime because the police would use the profile to develop suspects from innocent citizens that reside within their jurisdiction. In other words, the FBI profiler (driver) who is able to look out of his/her rear view mirror only is likely to cause some accidents.

In addition to the problems of investigator inexperience and the use of ineffective profiles, Dr. John Douglas, the Retired Former Head of the FBI's

Behavioral Science Unit and a board certified member of the American College of Forensic Examiners, indicates that if the local police unit is assisted by other investigative agencies there may be a competitive tug-of-war for evidence and information may not be shared. In short, the investigation of murder as a business decision is likely to also be characterized by significant investigative inefficiency in the form of information loss. An unsolved homicide is practically a certain consequence of offender experience on the one hand and investigator inefficiency and inexperience on the other.

Even though murder as a business decision has the potential for extensive individual and social harm, smaller police jurisdictions with crime mixes that are unlikely to include many business-like murders would receive, on the average, very little benefit from increased investigator training in economic reasoning. In the unlikely event that a business-like murder occurs in a smaller police jurisdiction it is, however, important that the crime be recognized for what it is and that specialized resources be available to assist in the investigation. Specialized investigative resources that could help in these types of cases are currently limited. Speaking from extensive experience with the FBI, Dr. John Douglas suggests that "flying squads" of specially trained experts may be a solution. For example, Dr. Douglas is currently the team leader for the Major Case Response Team (a "flying squad" of forensic experts) of the American College of Forensic Examiners.

Unfortunately, even with the availability of forensic expert "flying squads" the hole in the police dragnet may not be closed. This is because there are not a lot of forensic experts that are trained in the investigation of murder as a business decision. The overrepresentation of other non-economic theories of crime and criminal behavior may still lead to investigator bias. In the extreme absence of economic forensic representation all production processes would be non-economic. Moreover, production isoquants that related economic and non-economic forensic inputs to the solution (output) of murder as a business decision would consist only of points along the non-economic axis. Accordingly, all cost minimization or maximum output solutions would be corner solutions along the non-economic axis. Moreover, because non-economic theories of crime and criminal behaviors are unlikely to have significant, positive marginal values in murder as a business decision they may all be technically inefficient. Therefore, solutions (output) would always remain near zero for any level of cost.

THE RISK OF CONVICTION

The probability or risk of conviction is an important variable that is often assumed constant when analyzing other outputs such as the risk of arrest and the level of punishment. The relative importance of the risk of conviction is indicated in a study by Jeffrey Grogger (1991).[6] This study indicates that, for young male arrestees, the probability of conviction has a much larger deterrent effect than the level of punishment. Interestingly, empirical evidence presented by James Andreoni (1995) indicates that increasing the level of punishment (f) will have a negative impact on conviction probabilities.[7] Thus the assumption that the probability of conviction is held constant when varying the level of punishment (f) is not likely to be observed without the use of statistical procedures. According to Andreoni increasing the level of punishment (f) may influence conviction probabilities through two distinct channels. First, it may cause criminals to increase efforts to avoid detection and conviction. This is the "avoidance" effect. Second, it may increase the threshold level of reasonable doubt by juries because of the increased cost of an incorrect conviction. This is the "reasonable doubt" effect. Together these two effects may be strong enough to offset the deterrent effect of increased levels of punishment (f).

It may be that the "avoidance" and "reasonable doubt" effects that result from increased levels of punishment (f) will vary in importance and significance among different types of homicides. Consider the "avoidance" effect first. For rationally motivated homicides, increasing the level of punishment (f) is likely to result in a very strong "avoidance" effect. The predictable increase in effort toward apprehension and conviction avoidance on the part of rationally motivated homicide offenders must result in a direct increase in the cost of the homicide alternative. Increased costs and changes in the number and/or type of activities related to apprehension risk reduction may be difficult for non-offenders to observe. On the other hand, reducing the conditional risk of conviction may include observable factors such as increased expenditures and/or activities related to witness intimidation, witness murder, witness bribery, jury tampering, and better lawyers. If successful, as was often the case with John Gotti, conviction risk may be reduced to near zero. Moreover, the offender cannot be retried on the same offense once a "not guilty" verdict has been reached regardless of which method is used. For murder as a business decision, the avoidance effect due to expected decreases in apprehension probability (p) and the conditional risk of conviction is likely to outweigh the deterrent effect of increased punishment (f). Therefore, for rationally motivated homicide offenders, an increase only in punishment (f) may result in a net decrease in deterrence. It makes more sense to increase the level of punishment (f) and simultaneously increase the risks of apprehension (p) and conviction. The "avoidance" effect from increased (f) may then result in apprehension and conviction risks remaining relatively constant.

If the level of punishment (f) was significantly increased only for emotionally motivated or rashly committed homicides then the "avoidance" effect would, on the average, be more limited. This is because emotionally motivated homicides, if detected soon enough, are expected to be characterized by greater evidence availability. Since apprehension risk (p) would necessarily be greater the "avoidance" effect would be limited more to activities and expenditures related to reducing the risk of conviction. Conviction avoidance for emotionally motivated homicides would still be costly to the defendant. The O. J. Simpson case illustrates the level of expenses necessary to reduce the risk of conviction to near zero in such cases. To minimize the "avoidance" effect and maximize deterrence production, it appears to make more sense to increase the level of punishment (f) relatively more for emotionally motivated homicides.

Now consider the "reasonable doubt" effect. For rationally motivated or business-like homicides, it is not clear that a significant "reasonable doubt" effect would offset an increase in the level of punishment (f). If apprehended, a callus, rationally calculating and wealth seeking homicide offender should not expect a jury's sympathy. On the other hand, for emotionally motivated homicides in which the victim has previously abused the offender, there may be a significant offsetting "reasonable doubt" effect from increased levels of punishment (f). Although not a homicide, the Lorena Bobbitt case serves as an example. The jury found the defendant not guilty of amputating her husband's penis based on the irresistible impulse defense. Although the irresistible impulse defense was considered an "insanity" defense, powerful emotions would not have been considered an insanity defense. For the purposes of illustrating the "reasonable doubt" effect, however, the difference between emotional motivation and an irresistible impulse is not important. The irresistible impulse defense (recognized only in Colorado, Georgia, New Mexico, and Virginia) was presented by the defense merely a means for the jury to spare the defendant from punishment and deportation. Apparently the jury refused to convict because they believed that the defendant had already suffered enough punishment at the hands of the victim.

Holding the probability of arrest constant, a significant "reasonable doubt" effect that decreases the probability of conviction creates a large gap between the absolute value of punishment and the expected value of punishment. It is interesting to note also that the psychological evaluation in the Lorena Bobbitt case indicates that rational calculation was a significant aspect of the motivation to act as opposed to only an irresistible impulse.[8] In other words, an apparently emotionally motivated crime (such as an assault or homicide) may still involve a significant degree of rational calculation by the offender. Thus it may be that Lorena Bobbitt also took advantage of an opportunity in the form of an expected "reasonable doubt" effect. It seems reasonable to assume that an individual is less likely to resist (through rational calculation) the impulse of significant negative emotions if there is the perception of a significant "reasonable doubt" effect. This places significant importance on the production of convictions by courts. Perhaps the "reasonable doubt" effect in cases of abused and emotionally motivated homicide offenders can be abated if the insanity defense becomes more limited and unanimous jury verdicts are no longer required.

At first, this policy may seem very harsh. However, this issue is not whether an abused offender deserves more punishment. Rather, the issue is to deter crimes such as assaults and homicides. Deterring emotionally motivated homicides on the one hand and allocating resources to prevent abuse and to treat those who are abused on the other hand are two separate issues. As is often the case, such a policy is likely to cause other off-setting changes. Increasing punishment in order to deter emotionally motivated and abused offenders from committing homicides may, for example, increase the demand for more resources to prevent abuse and treat those who are abused. Thus, in a broader context, the policy may actually be much less harsh than it first appears.

Plea bargaining can also effect the probability of conviction. In the short-run, plea bargaining is often seen as a pragmatic and efficient way to resolve criminal cases because costly prosecutions are avoided and conviction (on a lesser charge) is guaranteed. This process seems to be reasonable for murder as a business decision because the level of punishment is less important to deterrence. Even though it may mean less punishment, it is reasonable to expect that there will be net gains in deterrence through increases in the risks of apprehension and conviction if the prosecutor can use plea bargaining as a means of obtaining testimony against other defendants that may be involved in a rationally motivated homicide.

For emotionally motivated homicides in which the offender is likely to be more sensitive to the level of punishment, reducing the level of punishment (f) through plea bargaining is likely to result in a net loss in deterrence. Therefore, plea bargaining (i.e., reduced punishment) in cases involving emotionally motivated homicides should only be used if the "reasonable doubt" and/or "avoidance" effects are likely to be significant.

Since most homicides appear to be emotionally motivated, the long-run consequences of plea bargaining, and hence net deterrence losses, will be to over-run society and the courts with criminal cases. This trend is already apparent. The only way to reverse this trend is to stop plea bargaining in those cases involving risk averse offenders in which there are no significant "reasonable doubt" or "conviction avoidance" effects expected. In the court system the long-run benefits of fewer cases will eventually outweigh the short-run costs of increased case loads. In the prison system emotionally motivated offenders would be incarcerated for much longer periods of time. However, in the long-run the total number of incarcerated offenders may be less if the deterrence effect of increased punishment (f) is strong enough. In any case, it seems reasonable to suppose that society will be better-off with fewer homicides.

ADDITIONAL OUTPUTS: REHABILITATION AND INCAPACITATION

Rehabilitation requires changing the tastes and preferences of an offender. In other words, if an offender (who is assumed rational) is expected to make different action choices, then the offender's objectives must be changed. The fact that criminal rehabilitation efforts have yet to show that they work adds support to the economic assumption of consistent tastes and preferences. Because younger offenders are influenced by legitimate alternatives, some types of job training programs may be more productive than rehabilitation. Job training does not change offender preferences but simply provides the means for offenders to choose among a larger set of wealth gaining alternatives. At the margin, this should increase the opportunity cost of crime and, thereby, lower the crime rate somewhat.

Some would argue that if professional criminal offenders cannot be reformed or retrained, then they must be permanently incarcerated or executed. In other words, incapacitation is argued to be the only way to decrease the number of crimes that professional criminals commit. This is not true. It has been shown that professional criminal offenders, who can be assumed rational, tend to be highly sensitive to changes in the risk of apprehension and, secondly, to the risks of conviction and/or punishment. Consequently, professional criminal offenders can be effectively deterred from committing crimes by increasing these risks. The problem with producing incapacitation is essentially the same as for increasing the level of punishment (f). Producing incapacitation is likely to cause professional criminals to put even more effort into reducing apprehension and conviction risks. Therefore, if the criminal justice system attempts to produce incapacitation as a public safety output in the case of professional criminals, it may find that apprehension and conviction is harder to achieve and the net effect of incapacitation on deterrence may actually be negative.

SUGGESTED READINGS.

1. Andreoni, J. "Criminal Deterrence in the Reduced Form: A New Perspective on Ehrlich's Seminal Study," *Economic Inquiry* 33 (July 1995): 476-483.

2. Ehrlich, I. "Crime, Punishment, and the Market for Offenses," *Journal of Economic Perspectives* 10 (Winter 1996): 43-67.

3. Grogger, J. "Certainty VS. Severity of Punishment," *Economic Inquiry* 29 (April 1991): 297-309.

CHAPTER 8
SUMMARY AND PRINCIPLE CONCLUSIONS

People (or any other biological organisms) respond to opportunities that are available to them. All else held constant, consumers buy more at lower prices and producers produce more at higher prices. For professional offenders the relatively low risk of apprehension and conviction for murder as a business decision means that this crime is likely to be common. In response to the crime of murder as a business decision, as well as crime in general, society and the criminal justice system must first be educated about the effectiveness of negative incentives to crime as an aspect of deterrence. This is critical because professional criminals already understand the importance of deterrence. For example, an article in *The Arizona Republic* that refers to the June 2, 1976 bombing attack on Arizona Republic investigative reporter Don Bolles quotes then attorney general Bruce Babbit as saying that it was "an incredibly brazen attempt to intimidate everybody working on the problem of organized crime and corruption."[1]

Assuming that the law abiding aspect of society and the criminal justice system can also appreciate the need for deterrence it is important that the resulting decrease in crime rates not be penalized by a reduction in criminal justice system resources. Changing the level of resources to match the crime rate creates perverse incentives for law enforcement. In other words, if successfully reducing the crime rate is expected to lead to fewer resources and an increase in the crime rate is expected to lead to more resources then law enforcement will be, in effect, deterred from producing an output.

Some methods of deterrence cannot be legislated. In the case of rationally motivated offenders, the risk of apprehension (p) must be increased and this requires that criminal investigators understand economic reasoning. In the case of murder as a business decision increased efforts by those not trained in economic reasoning are more likely to be counter productive. Non-economic theories may lead police away from the true offender and decrease the risk of apprehension and conviction.

Clearly, there is no incentive to be a witness in cases involving murder as a business decision--unless, of course, one wants to be targeted for murder and enter the witness protection program. Moreover, there is also no incentive for a witness to want to run through a gauntlet of criminal psychologists. Although criminal psychologists may be given the task of evaluating a witness and trying to determine whether the witness is telling the truth a witness who is telling the truth can not trust this process. For example, one of the reasons that Richard Jewell was considered the prime suspect in Atlanta's Centennial Park bombing was due to the perception by criminal psychologists that he might be lying. In essence, the indisputable fact that it was physically impossible for Mr. Jewell to have committed the bombing was exchanged for psychological speculation. As a consequence, Richard Jewell's career was ruined and he suffered severe economic and, probably, psychological damages.

In some cases, such as the Centennial Park bombing, a potential witness may perceive that there is very little distinction between a criminal organization seeking to harm members of society and a criminal justice system that wants to clear a case by whatever means appears to be the easiest. All forms of witness deterrence will surely decrease the probabilities of apprehension, conviction, and punishment for murder as a business decision.

The only incentive to become a witness is when an opportunity presents itself to easily apprehend an offender (and possible get a reward) or, perhaps, to apprehend criminal justice system investigators who are caught perpetrating wrongs. Also, a selfless individual might be willing to incur the costs of becoming a witness if his or her moral values are strong enough. When a witness is motivated to apprehend criminal investigators who are perpetrating social wrongs it is likely to result in quite a battle. This appears to be true even when the witness is an undercover police officer such as Frank Serpico. The witness must be prepared to win the battle if net gains are to be achieved.

There is also the possibility that some criminal offenders will act as a witness in an attempt to throw off investigators. Obviously, the motives of these individuals should not be confused with the motives of actual witnesses.

Interestingly, the situation in which investigators must determine if a witness is telling the truth or should be treated as a suspect should be expected to result more often when criminal profiles or psychological conjecture forms the basis of an investigation. Again, considering the Olympic Park Bombing case, if professional terrorists planted the bomb it is possible that someone such as a security guard like Richard Jewell, or even someone else, may have seen one or more of the offenders near the crime scene. Since such offenders want to avoid apprehension they can be expected to keep a low profile and the witness may not initially connect them with the crime. Once a psychological based criminal profile or psychological conjecture create a theoretical suspect--which, because he or she was near the crime scene, may be the witness--the witness may become more focused on the crime that he or she is now unexpectedly involved in and remember enough to be able to associate the observed offenders with the crime.[2] Reporting these facts to investigators subsequent to becoming labeled a suspect, which the suspect would be obligated to do, would obviously create a difficult situation. Investigators would then have to try to verify or refute the witnesses reported "facts." This may be difficult or impossible if professional offenders are involved. On the other hand, psychologists and/or profilers who are motivated to show that their speculation or conjecture is actually right, probably in the face of obvious factual contradictions, may continue and continue to plague the witness.

If criminal investigators cannot distinguish between crime scenes that are staged by rationally motivated homicide offenders and crime scenes that are actually the result of emotionally motivated offenders then it is difficult to expect that the criminal justice system can increase the levels of apprehension and conviction risk for murder as a business decision. It is also more difficult to argue for increasing the level of punishment and, hence, deterrence for emotionally motivated homicides. There would be a significant increase in social harm if innocent persons who just happen to fit one or more aspects of an erroneous and subjectively applied criminal profile became the primary suspects of a crime that was actually committed by highly experienced, professional offenders.

It is also important that criminal investigators understand the economic ramifications of investigating organized crime. By attempting to increase the risk of apprehension, conviction, and punishment, criminal investigators may have the effect of decreasing the expected value of traditional income flows to criminal organizations. As it was with the end of prohibition and later with gambling casinos in Cuba and then gambling casinos in Nevada, criminal organizations do not simply disappear along with their traditional source of income. Instead, they look for new criminal opportunities. 'Big money' or 'no money' gambles are the types of opportunities expected to be sought. These types of opportunities are consistent with preferences for risk and the von Neumannn--Morgenstern utility function. That such opportunities would be sought in response to a criminal investigation is a fact that was shown to be mathematically predictable. Obviously, predictable behavior on the part of organized crime such as this could be used by law enforcement to set up "sting" operations that are specifically designed to entrap members of criminal organizations. Law enforcement would be negligent if it failed to implement pro-active "sting" operations that prevented predictable homicides from occurring.[3]

There is a "hole in the police dragnet" through which rationally motivated and experienced homicide offenders routinely pass. The rationally motivated homicide profile developed in chapter 6 emphasized gains in information from planning and criminal experience and gains from organizational specialization through the involvement of multiple offenders. Accordingly, the profile assumed that rationally motivated homicides comprised all youth gang killings, gangland killings, institutional offenders, sniper attacks, and felony homicides. Thus rationally motivated homicides are assumed to represent approximately one-third of all homicides. Other data indicates that about one-fifth of all homicides are associated with youth gang killings.[4] This heavily weights rationally motivated homicides toward youth gang killings. Moreover, youth gang killings have tended to increase in numbers and in proportion to other homicides over time.

Youth gangs are defined to consist of juveniles between the ages of 10 to 22 years of age. Of this group most are in the 18 to 22 year old range and have been arrested more than once. Prior arrests, for only a small fraction of delinquent behavior, indicate that youth gang members are highly experienced criminals. Being organized into a 'gang' indicates that the members often act in a coordinated and planned manner and gain efficiency from organizational specialization. In other words, youth gangs can be considered to be "junior" organized crime. Youth gangs can therefore be expected to maintain secrecy about criminal activities (through loyalty to each other or through intimidation), harass or execute witnesses as necessary, pick-up evidence, and conduct planned homicides (for example, drive-by-shootings) in the pursuit of wealth related objectives that may involve territory and/or criminal enterprise.

Because rational calculation is indicated to be a causal a factor in homicides, it is reasonable to expect that rationally motivated offenders, including youth gangs, will continue to consider homicide an alternative. Moreover, since rationality implies that offenders learn how to exploit homicide as an alternative, it is likely that rationally motivated homicides will tend to increase over time. Whether considered separately or as inter-related factors, rationally motivation and increased youth gang activity appear to be among the primary explanatory factors for homicide clearance rates that have diminished from over 90% in 1960 to approximately 60% to 65% today.

Mending this "hole in the dragnet" is not a simple task. There appear to be two main avenues to follow. One avenue involves a better understanding of the economic and social forces that influence youth gang activity. Thus sociologists can be expected to play a major role. However, making society safer for citizens and the police is not equivalent to improving the efficiency and effectiveness of police production. The police "dragnet" refers to planned police procedures for pursuing and catching offenders. In other words, the "hole in police dragnet" can only be mended if there is an improvement in police investigative production. Improving police homicide investigation production is quintessential to mending the hole in the police dragnet.

Improving the effectiveness and efficiency of police investigative production in the area of rationally motivated homicide offenders involves improving technology, changing attitudes and beliefs about crime and criminal behavior, and changing the level of resources aimed at solving this type of homicide. Changes in police technology through more extensive education and training in economic theory will directly improve the productivity of investigative resources.[5] For example, police investigators need to have a better understanding of the nature of economic models, economic models of crime and criminal behavior, and the implications of risk preferences to offender behavior.

It also appears that improving investigative production in the area of rationally motivated homicides will require a change in attitudes and beliefs about crime and criminal behavior. Attitudes and beliefs manifest themselves as preferences for suspects with certain behavior and demographic characteristics. This makes it more difficult to apprehend business-like murderers who are less likely to have the desired characteristics. In other words, attitudes and beliefs place an upper limit on the extent that police investigative technology can be improved.

Changing attitudes and beliefs will be a difficult task because it involves everyone from academicians to those directly involved in law enforcement. It may be that academicians not trained in economics are among those who have the most entrenched attitudes and beliefs--especially regarding homicide. Regarding murder as a business decision, non-economic academicians may even subject economists to some form of "academic inquisition." At least among police, increased training in economic theory should help overcome the attitude and belief hurdle.

Assuming technically efficient resource utilization, the reallocation of resources within the criminal justice system may still be required to achieve production or cost efficiency and increase investigative output. For example, there are few economists but many criminal psychologists employed by units of the criminal justice system. In the garbage truck production example in Chapter 4 this would be like producing output (assumed to be technically efficient) with all labor and no truck or with one truck and no labor. Obviously, output should increase with a more balanced use of resources.

Unfortunately, technical efficiency in criminal justice system production is difficult to assume. Regarding only the homicide investigation aspect of criminal justice system production, there is really no consensus on the best way to carry out the many activities related to homicide investigation. Without technical efficiency, production (cost) efficiency is impossible to obtain. In other words, the "hole in the police dragnet" is equivalent to saying that there is a fall in output per unit of input due to possible technical inefficiency.

In part, technical inefficiency must be suspected because of the debate concerning the use of outside or augmentative resources in homicide investigation. This debate is predicated on the fact that some local police units are known to be technically inefficient when it comes to homicide investigations--or at least some types of homicide investigations. Putting issues related to experience aside, it is often suggested that there may be new technologies that have yet to be implemented and that will lead to improvements in criminal justice system efficiency and the increased production of apprehension and conviction for homicide. For example, the increased use of specialized "flying squads" composed of forensic experts appears promising. On the other hand, the likely under-representation of economics among forensic specialists remains troubling. Moreover, it is not clear theoretically or empirically that psychological or criminal profiles as developed by the FBI are a productive input in criminal investigations involving rationally motivated offenders.[6]

More generally, the increase in psychological behavior training of police officers may, on the average, actually result in investigative obscurantism. For example, factual investigative information may be more often wrongly questioned on the basis of psychological conjecture. As in the Atlanta Centennial Park bombing, police investigators may trade away facts (e.g., the suspect could not have done it) for conjecture (e.g., a criminal psychologist theorizes that the witness/suspect is lying). In this way, criminal investigators are actually buying technical inefficiency. That psychological conjecture contradicted by obvious fact is illogical and, if acted on, must result in technical efficiency is perhaps an understatement. It is imbecilic!

In the TV program *DRAGNET* police sergeant Joe Friday was often noted to be interested in obtaining just the facts and only the facts. Sgt. Friday was clearly not interested in witness conjecture. Today, witness conjecture may come as police conjecture that has its basis in psychological behavior training. Similar to witness conjecture police conjecture may more often than not obscure the facts. If psychological/criminal profiles and/or psychological behavior training are technically inefficient they must necessarily contribute to falling homicide clearance rates. It may be that technical efficiency in homicide investigation was more closely achieved in the 1960s when the homicide clearance rates were above 90%. In those days, *DRAGNET* was popular and criminal profiles and psychological behavior training was not the current fad.

A way to test whether psychological input into criminal investigations is an explanatory factor in falling homicide clearance rates would be to divide homicide cases to be investigated and homicide investigators into two groups. Investigative output would be the percentage of homicide convictions achieved within a year.[7] One group of investigators would not use profiles or be specifically trained in psychology. This group would be expected to determine the facts in each case and then determine which competing explanation for those facts was correct. This is the "Sherlock Holmes" approach. The other group of investigators would be specifically trained in psychology and in the use of criminal profiles. This would be the "Mind Hunter" approach.[8] If the first group of homicide investigators obtains a significantly higher percentage of convictions within the year then it should be clear that technical inefficiency explains why homicide clearance rates are currently at such a low level.

Another way to understand the importance of technical inefficiency in the context of police homicide clearance rate production is by analogy. Assuming that the "Mind Hunter" approach to homicide investigation turns out to be less efficient it would be because this process is not the best. This would indicate technical inefficiency of the "Mind Hunters." Technical inefficiency would occur because factual information would be augmented by information in the form of theory, conjecture, and speculation. All information must be checked and either refuted and verified. However, processing and checking the additional "information" would absorb investigative resources at a high rate and/or prolong investigations. The analogy is that "technical inefficiency of the mind" due to psychological problems that inhibit information processing also explains why some individuals achieve only a low level of utility -- such as many of those who live in the street. It is true that those who live in the street may also be addicted to some drugs that, given meager resources, constrains the number of alternatives available for consideration. Similarly, a criminal justice system addicted to the fad of criminal profiles is limited in terms of applicable investigative techniques to consider if resource constraints are an issue.

The analogy should not be extended so far as to suggest that the criminal justice system is similar to and, therefore, can only interact with offenders who live in the street. Although one should note that such a prediction is consistent with the general characteristics of a large proportion of convicted offenders. On the other hand, the potential social tyranny suggested by the earlier blind driver/profiler analogy and the potential for negative productivity when psychologists and/or profilers deter witnesses and/or unwittingly aid rationally motivated homicide offenders suggests that perhaps the word "elite" does not mean what the FBI thinks it means when it describes its behavioral science unit.

Unfortunately, technical inefficiency of the "mind hunters" involves predominantly a public sector production process and is, therefore, less likely to soon disappear. If such an operation occurred in the private sector, or was without any public sector demand, it would probably not last long. Imagine, for example, an enterprise called "mind shoppers." Instead of spending time going through a grocery store, reading labels and comparing prices "mind shoppers" would offer to do this task for a fee. Of course you still have to pay for your groceries as before. "Mind shoppers" would quickly assess your personality and develop a shopper profile for you and then use this information as the basis for making your consumer choices and filling your shopping cart. If, on the average, shoppers do not get exactly what they want (i.e., they gain less than optimal utility) then "mind shoppers" would, of course, go out of business. In this case, "mind shoppers" would be considered a technically inefficient shopping process such that some consumers end-up paying for a "hole in their shopping cart." If "mind shoppers" operated in the public sector, on the other hand, it could then go on producing little or no output as long as it continued to be subsidized. Perhaps a way to put a public sector "mind shopper" operation out of business is to seize upon an opportunity to hunt it down and expose its inefficiency in a manner that cannot be ignored.

Whether it is legitimate market activity or not, market efficiency is a tough thing with which to compete. Rational calculation that occurs prior to a homicide event suggests planning, coordinated and specialized efforts by the offenders involved. Private production, whether legitimate or not, usually means that the benefits of a business like organization or "firm" can be more fully exploited. Thus youth gangs, gangland offenders, and terrorist groups can benefit from specialization and economies of scale. Moreover, business management courses teach us that once an organization exists rational calculation is necessary to fully exploit the benefits. Thus rational calculation that leads to the creation of a criminal organization is itself in greater demand once the organization comes into existence. Nevertheless, the goal of criminal justice system production should always be to drive rational, professional and organized homicide offenders out of business. Doing this will help reverse the trend of falling homicide clearance rates.

As indicated, sociological research aimed at understanding youth gangs appears to be necessary as one of the avenues toward achieving this goal. In addition to investigative production, the police role involves increasing homicide deterrence effectiveness. To be sure, improvements in investigative production will directly contribute to the deterrence of rationally motivated offenders who tend to be more sensitive to changes in the risk of apprehension. However, attempts at changing attitudes and beliefs about crime and criminal behavior through changes in police training curriculums, the increased use of quick response teams of forensic examiners, sociological research concerning youth gangs and the elimination of technically inefficient production processes are only some of the steps needed. In order to combat the benefits of organized criminal homicide, significant institutional reform that increases the level of resources toward homicide investigation appears to also be necessary. For example, institutional reforms might include making all homicides that are not cleared by arrest within a specified period of time, such as 60 days, subject to review by criminal investigators at the State level. The State crime unit could decide to take over the case at that point. After 120 days Federal authorities could begin a review process and decide whether to take over a case--either from State or local officials. This would put pressure on local authorities to solve their homicides. A possible consequence of increased pressure to solve homicides might be the increased use of additional specialized resources in more investigations.[9] Increase solution pressure may also limit political forces that in some cases lead to cover-ups.

Bringing Federal authorities into a homicide investigation that would otherwise not be subject to Federal jurisdiction would allow Federal investigators to gain much broader experience and increase their level of productivity in homicide investigations. Currently, Federal investigators tend to interview only a limited set of homicide offenders such as serial-killers, sexual-killers, and assassins. Projecting this limited and biased experience into a homicide investigation could very well play into the hands of rationally motivated offenders. This appears to be the case in Atlanta's Centennial Olympic Park bombing that occurred on July 27, 1996. Professional terrorists have now become the prime suspects.

Institutional reform such as this would increase both the level and productivity of resources aimed at clearing homicides. Currently, increased investigative resources are assured only when homicides appear to involve organized crime and terrorist groups. Increased levels of investigative resources should also be allocated toward youth gang related homicides. Regardless of the level and trend of youth gang activity, this should increase homicide clearance rates significantly. Deterring rationally motivated offenders through increased clearance rates and emotionally motivated offenders through greater levels of punishment should further increase homicide clearance rates by reducing the workload. Of course, there should also be consideration given to the level of resources available for prosecution and to court production (cost) efficiency.[10] It does little to arrest an offender if there is no credible risk of conviction.

Institutional reform that involves greater levels of investigative resources and the use of technologies such as quick response teams of forensic experts cannot escape the short-run economic problem of diminishing returns to variable factors. This would be an acute problem in homicide cases where a large number of similarly trained investigative experts become involved. There are three ways to offset the effect of diminishing returns. One way is to increase the training and level of productivity of the investigative factors of production, a second way is to use investigative experts that are more diversified in their training and area of expertise, and a third way is to use fewer experts. The gain in marginal productivity from using fewer experts is equivalent to saying that those investigators who arrive at the crime scene first are likely to be the most productive. This also suggests that investigators who are first on the crime scene (who may be patrol officers) should be among those who receive the most education and training in homicide investigation and who are among those actively involved in the investigation.

What about police units that believe they need not fear the occurrence of homicides committed by professional offenders such as with organized crime? Let them recall the bank robbery career of Bonnie and Clyde during the early 1930's. The Barrow gang intentionally picked on small rural banks because there was a lower risk of apprehension. They also killed 12 people. As professional bank robbers and homicide offenders the Barrow gang was apparently more concerned with minimizing the risk of apprehension than with maximizing the level of wealth gains because their most productive robbery gained them only $3,500.00.

Small towns are easy pickings for organized crime today also. A major difference is that when Bonnie and Clyde came to town you knew who they were. Today, crime scene staging and the probably lack of evidence means that small town police units will not know who did it. As with the chances of being killed by the Barrow gang the probability of any other professionally committed homicide occurring in a small town is low. On the other hand, not all youth gang activity is confined to large cities. Moreover, the hypothetical example in chapter 4 indicated that all it takes to motivate professional homicide offenders is just one individual who holds the key to an economic opportunity that might be exploited by organized crime.

As indicated, the occurrence of a professionally committed homicide in a small town means that involving the FBI behavioral science unit in the investigation will only further reduce the chances of apprehension and conviction. The criminal profile for rationally motivated homicides developed in Chapter 6 indicates that, given the lack of substantial evidence, there are two methods that may help identify professional homicide offenders. The first method involves determining whether anyone benefited from the homicide. It may be difficult to identify all offenders this way because (due to circumstances that are different and often changing) opportunity costs can be negative for some offenders. When this is so even a benefit level of zero can still be associated with a homicide that is a rational decision. Once a field of suspects is identified using the first method the second method, which involves using the risk of apprehension and conviction, can be implemented. Since the homicide is planned, the offenders expect to get away with it and varying the level of punishment is not, therefore, expected to be a concern to such offenders. Varying the risk of punishment through increases in the risk of apprehension and conviction is, on the other hand, likely to be a big concern. It is likely that rationally motivated homicide offenders will make every attempt to avoid the source of the increased risk of apprehension and punishment. Avoidance actions should be helpful in identifying the offenders.

Choice theory also suggests that rationally motivated homicide offender(s) must be callous toward the victim(s). Otherwise they may not consider homicide just another alternative.

A caveat to the use of these techniques is that it is better to use whatever real evidence is available when varying the risk of apprehension and punishment. Professional homicide offenders are among those most likely to believe that "no-one lies like a cop." Moreover, the use of real evidence is preferable to the unlikely hypotheses of existing criminal profiles.

NOTES

CHAPTER ONE

1.   Even consumers pronounced irrational in some sense, such as chronic psychotics at a New York State mental institution, showed that psychotics obey the law of demand, that is, they too buy less when prices are raised, etc. See R. C. Battalio et al., "A Test of Consumer Demand Theory Using Observations of Individual Purchases," *Western Economic Journal* (December 1973): 411-428.

2.   An abstract economic model is one that is made less realistic (and complex) through the use of simplifying assumptions.   However, in the context of the problem to be analyzed, the most important aspects of reality should still remain in the model.   "Rational Economic Man" is an example of such an abstraction. "Rational economic man" refers to that aspect of behavior (rationality) that allows for prediction in economic models.   Reality is more complicated or, equivalently, less abstract.   For example, emotions (and the way the it influences choices) are less predictable.

3.   Actually, money is not a resource.   Resources, for example labor and capital equipment, must be real, physical contributors to production output.   In this example, money is simply a representative measure of the value of a consumer's labor (the actual resource) within the context of an institutional structure such as a competitive market.

CHAPTER TWO

1.   The marginal product of labor (MPL) is calculated as the change in output (Q) divided by the change in the variable input (L) with all other inputs assumed to be held constant.   By letting Δ represent "change in" the MPL = $\Delta Q/\Delta L$.

Assuming that both ΔQ and ΔL are > 0, if $\Delta Q > \Delta L$ then MPL is increasing and if $\Delta Q < \Delta L$ then MPL is positive but diminishing.

2.   Even in competitive industries or markets economic profits can exist in the short-run because firms do not have time to enter or leave.

CHAPTER THREE

1.   The marginal cost curves may actually slope or curve upwards if the chances of getting a ticket increase with each mph of excessive speed above the legal limit. If this is so, the optimal choice for mph of illegal speed will be less.

2.   See B. B. Hull and F. Bold, "Preaching Matters: Replication and Extension," *Journal of Economic Behavior and Organization* 27 (June 1995): 143-149.

3.   In contrast, constant marginal utility for each mph of excessive speed indicates an indifference to risky driving and increasing marginal utility for each mph of excessive speed indicates that an individual actually prefers risky behavior when driving.

4.   See, for example, Darrough, M. N. and J. M. Heineke, *The Multi-Output Translog Production Cost Function: The Case of Law Enforcement Agencies* (In *Economic Models of Criminal Behavior*, ed. J. M. Heineke, 259-302. Amsterdam: North Holland, 1978).

5.   Because increasing drug enforcement re-allocates police resources it may lead to increases in property crime by reducing deterrence to property crime. Moreover, increases in drug arrests and the property crime rate are positively correlated with police resources. See Sollars, Benson, and Rasmussen, "Drug Enforcement and the Deterrence of Property Crime Among Local Jurisdictions," *Public Finance Quarterly* 22 (January 1994): 22-45.

6.   Bounded rationality means that fewer alternatives may be generated and considered or, equivalently, that less information about alternatives and

consequences is processed. With imperfect information an individual cannot attempt to optimize but must simply "satisfice" or do the best that is possible given the circumstances or his or her mental state.

CHAPTER FOUR

1. See M. K. Block and J. Heineke, "A Labor Theoretical Analysis of the Criminal Choice," *American Economic Review* 65 (June 1975): 314-325.

2. By engaging in activities such as creating a "mole" organized crime clearly indicates the importance of apprehension/conviction risk reduction or, equivalently, a high level of sensitivity to risk. Creating a "mole" is also similar to activities associated with military intelligence. Moreover, military intelligence activities are assumed to be based exclusively on rational calculation.

3. Crime scenes may be staged or not depending on the specific objectives of organized crime. For example, if a warning to other individuals is intended then the homicide may clearly indicate a professional hit. On the other hand, the objective of making Mr. X a "mole" requires that the crime scene be staged to look like some other type of homicide that does not involve organized crime.

4. The numerical values can be changes substantially and murder is still likely to remain the best choice.

5. The three equations are from G. Becker, "Crime and Punishment: An Economic Approach," *Journal of Political Economy* 76 (March-April 1968): 169-217.

6. $\partial EU/\partial p = U(G - f) - U(G) < 0$, assuming that $f > 0$. Also, $\partial EU/\partial f = -pU'(G-f) < 0$ if the marginal utility of wealth remains positive. One might also note that when rational calculation results in $p = 0$, the significance of f becomes irrelevant (i.e., $\partial EU/\partial f = 0$).

7. See, for example, D. A. Hellman and J. L. Naroff, *The Urban Public Sector and Urban Crime: A Simultaneous System Approach* (Washington: U. S.

Government Printing Office, 1980); S. F. Messner, "Regional Differences in the Economic Correlates of the Urban Homicide Rate: Some Evidence on the Importance of Cultural Context," *Criminology* 21 (November 1983): 177-188; and G. E. Marché, *The Economics of Law Enforcement: Production Comparisons Between Large and Small Police Unites* (Ann Arbor, Mich.: University Microforms, 1990).

8.   The disappearance of Jimmy Hoffa on July 31, 1975, serves as an example of the efficiency and certainty of a business-like murder in which organized crime is involved.

9.   Wealth gains from alternative (Y) may also become zero or negative due to a change in government policy, law, or even technology. For example, more efficient drug treatments and/or a change to a noncash economy might cause illegal drug suppliers to look for better alternatives. For individuals, negative opportunity costs (Y) can result from a change of circumstances. For example, a teenager may prefer to go home and study rather than to stay out with friends. However, if the teenager knows that his/her stepfather has just come home drunk and will probably be abusive then staying out with friends (even if they are trouble prone and, on average, provide a zero net gain in utility) may be the rational thing to do.

CHAPTER FIVE

1.   Even if professional hit-men are used to carry out a homicide and organized crime is involved so that secrecy can be enforced, the probability of apprehension is still (if only slightly) greater than zero.

2.   I. Ehrlich, "The Deterrent Effect of Capital Punishment: A Question of Life and Death," *American Economic Review* 65 (June 1975): 397-417.

3. This is done by letting price (P) – Pa, Pc|a, and Pe|c and quantity (Q) = U*, where U* represents the offender's expected utility from murder in the standard elasticity formula (see chapter 1).

4. From G. Becker, "Crime and Punishment: An Economic Approach," *Journal of Political Economy* 76 (March-April 1968): 169-217.

5. W. Furlong, "The Deterrent Effect of Regulatory Enforcement in the Fishery," *Land Economics* 67 (February 1991): 116-129.

6. Evidence suggests that today's crime prone boys are very present oriented in that they are incapable of deferring immediate gratification for the sake of future rewards. See, for example, M. Fleisher, *Beggars and Thieves* (Milwaukee: University of Wisconsin Press, 1995).

7. J. Q. Wilson, *Thinking About Crime* rev. ed. (New York: Basic Books, 1983), 137-42.

8. Of course organized, professional homicide offenders probably retain lawyers that are effective at reducing the risk of conviction given apprehension, the risk of punishment given conviction, and the level of punishment through means such as plea bargaining. For the criminal justice system, this would increase the cost of producing punishment (f) even if offenders placed the greatest emphasis on reducing apprehension risk (p). Unlike the unavoidable costs of production incurred by the criminal justice system, those offenders who successfully reduce apprehension risk (p) can avoid all subsequent costs associated with punishment (f) can be avoided.

9. Since risk-sensitive homicide offenders are assumed to be more rationally motivated, it follows that risk-averse (punishment-sensitive) homicide offenders can be assumed as less rationally (more emotionally) motivated. Emotionally motivated homicide offenders are expected to display less planning (or have less experience) and be less concerned with minimizing the risk of apprehension prior to committing the homicide. On the average, this should result in more evidence and a greater risk of apprehension. The differences in apprehension probabilities between rationally motivated and emotionally motivated homicides, all other

factors the same, appears to be about 17 percentage points. For example, if emotionally motivated homicides have a probability of being cleared by arrest of 67 percentage points then rationally motivated homicides have a probability of being cleared by arrest of 67 - 17 = 50 percentage points (i.e., p = 0.5). If hit-men are used such that there is no victim/offender relationship and there are gains from organizational specialization, the probability of a homicide being cleared by arrest drops by an additional 48 percentage points. Thus business-like murders that use hit-men have, on the average, a 65 percentage point decrease in the probability of being cleared by an arrest when compared to the more common emotionally motivated homicide in which there is usually a victim/offender relationship. See G. E. Marché, "The Production of Homicide Solutions: An Empirical Analysis," *American Journal of Economics and Sociology* 53 (October 1994): 385-401.

10.   In Japan, for example, murderers are said to act as if they expect to be caught. Not surprisingly, the murder clearance rate in Japan is almost 100%. Many observers have also commented that the behavior of the Japanese in general appears to consistently exhibit risk aversion. If Japanese murderers also tend to be risk-averse, economic theory predicts that the level of punishment (f) would be the only relevant (negative) deterrent.

11.   Data are based on revised Uniform Crime Reports; Characteristics of State Prisoners, 1960, table A1 and R3; and National Corrections Reporting Program, 1991, table 2.3.

12.   Of course, inexperienced investigators may be completely fooled by crime scene staging and incorrectly classify the homicide.

CHAPTER SIX

1.   The material in this chapter is based on an earlier publication by the author entitled "Mending a Hole in the Police Dragnet: A Criminal Profile for Rationally Motivated Homicides," *Forensics: TEJ* The Electronic On-line

211

Journal of the American College of Forensic Examiners (Spring 1996).

2.   A. J. Pinnizzotto and N. J. Finkel, "Criminal Personality Profiling: An Outcome and Process Study," *Law and Human Behavior* 14 (June 1990): 215-233.

3.   R. N. Turco, "Psychological Profiling," *International Journal of Offender Therapy and Comparative Criminology* 34, no. 2 (1990): 147-154.

4.   See J. T. McCann, "Criminal Personality Profiling in the Investigation of Violent Crime: Recent Advances and Future Directions," *Behavioral Sciences and the Law* 10, no. 4 (1992): 475-481.

5.   Turco, "Psychological Profiling."

6.   J. Douglas et al., "Criminal Profiling from Crime Scene Analysis," *Behavioral Sciences and the Law* 4, no. 4 (1986): 401- 421.

7.   See Douglas et al., "Criminal Profiling . . ." and W. Murphy and J. Peters, "Profiling Child Sexual Abuses: Psychological Considerations," *Criminal Justice and Behavior* 19 (March 1992): 24-37 and 38-53

8.   Hate crimes do not include homicides in which one individual kills another in an attempt to relieve hate when that emotion has arisen out of an interpersonal relationship. Hate crimes, including homicides, are those in which violence (which may actually be less emotionally motivated) is directed at a particular group of people of which the victim just happens to be a member.

9.   See Darrough and Heineke. *The Multi-Output Translog Production Cost Function: The Case of Law Enforcement Agencies* (In *Economic Models of Criminal Behavior*, ed. J. M. Heincke, 259-302. Amsterdam: North Holland, 1978).

10.   See G. E. Marché, "Aggregation Biases and Economies of Scale in the Metropolitan Police Unit Production Function," *Review of Social Economy* 1 (Summer 1992): 215-233.

11.   The offender file is used because it provides the greatest amount of offender information. There is one record (Observation) for each offender. Multiple victims are nested within offenders in the offender file and qualitative

characteristics are artificially invariant across all victims. However, multiple victims and multiple offenders occur in only three percent and four percent of the incidents, respectively, and the invariance of characteristics for multiple victims is not expected to affect the statistical inferences significantly.

12.   See, for example, R. B. Felson, "Impression Management and the Escalation of Aggression and Violence," *Social Psychology Quarterly* 45, no. 4 (1982): 245-254; Felson, Ribner and Siegel, "Age and the Effect of Third Parties During Criminal Violence," *Sociology and Social Research* 68, no. 4 (1984): 452-462; and Felson and Steadman, "Situational Factors in Disputes Leading to Criminal Violence," *Criminology* 21 (February 1983): 59-74.

13.   Crime and drug use are highly correlated. It is therefore likely that many emotionally motivated homicides are induced by drugs and/or alcohol.

14.   In terms of demand, a suboptimal choice would be when a consumer buys a good when the price (marginal cost) is greater than the marginal benefit. The consumer is then in the "irrational zone" on his or her demand curve.

15.   Investigators must take care that a crime scene has not been staged by professional business-like homicide offenders so that it appears that someone with severe mental, emotional, or information processing difficulties is the offender. In such cases business-like homicide offenders can expect that the police will be able to find someone who resides within their jurisdiction and who appears to be such an individual. Professional offenders also can expect that it would be easier for the police to "clear" a homicide by charging such an individual rather than to actually solve the crime. A relevant case occurred in 1986 in *Wilson v. Missouri.*

16.   "Unsolved" (UNS) is defined to mean that the offender remains unknown as reported in the monthly supplemental homicide reports (SHRs). "Solved" means that the offender is known and the homicide is assumed to then be cleared by an arrest. The assumption that "Solutions" equal "Clearances by arrest" is supported by the fact that the 1983 monthly SHR solution rates for homicide incidents are only slightly less (73.3%) than the annual 1983 UCR homicide incident clearance rate of 75.9%. The close approximation of monthly solution

rates and annual clearance rates appears to also suggest that the monthly SHRs are an accurate indicator of longer-run police investigator performance.

17.   See Marché, "The Production of Homicide Solutions . . . ," *American Journal of Economics and Sociology* 53 (October 1994): 385-401.

18.   See DiIulio, "The Black Crime Gap," *The Wall Street Journal*, 11 July 1994, sec. A, p. 10.

19.   See Kleck, "Racial Discrimination in Criminal Sentencing . . . ," *American Sociological Review* 46 (December 1981): 783-805.

20.   This suggests that crime scenes reflecting apparent spontaneity and/or disorganized murders in which there is no clear victim/offender relationship (VOR) should be examined with some degree of skepticism. See Ressler et al., "Sexual Killers and Their Victims . . . ," *Journal of Interpersonal Violence* 1 (September 1986): 288-253.

21.   Wilson, *Thinking About Crime* rev. ed., 137-42.

CHAPTER SEVEN

1.   G. Becker, *Accounting for Tastes* (Cambridge: Harvard University Press, 1996).

2.   Selling crack cocaine, for example, can generate as much as $100.00 a night, involves little or no work, and can be done while socializing with friends.

3.   There are, of course, additional consequences of failing to produce a sufficient amount of criminal deterrence. For example, repressive regimes all over the world use the level of crime and the number of firearm killings in the U. S. as a primary reason to not allow individual and political freedom.

4.   Marché, "The Production of Homicide Solutions . . . ," *American Journal of Economics and Sociology* 53 (October 1994): 385-401.

5.   The facts in this example are based on V. Scalice, "White House Counsel, Vincent Foster Case Reopened," *Forensic Examiner* 4 (September - October

1995): 13-15. Mr. Scalice is a Fellow of the American College of Forensic Examiners and Chairman, Executive Board of Scientific and Technical Advisors of the American Board of Forensic Examiners. The *Forensic Examiner* is the official publication of the American College of Forensic Examiners.

6.   J. Grogger, "Certainty v. Severity of Punishment," *Economic Inquiry* 29 (April 1991): 297-309.

7.   See J. Andreoni, "Criminal Deterrence in the Reduced Form: A New Perspective on Ehrlich's Seminal Study," *Economic Inquiry* 33 (July 1995): 476-483.

8.   M. R. Ryans, "The Irresistible Impulse in the Lorena Bobbitt Case," *Forensic Examiner* 5 (September - October 1996): 11-12. The *Forensic Examiner* is the official publication of the American College of Forensic Examiners.

CHAPTER EIGHT

1.   T. Kuhn, "Blast meant to intimidate, Babbit says," *The Arizona Republic*, 3 June 1976, sec. A., p. 19.

2.   If the crime is perpetrated in a small town or city everyone in residence (which will of course not include the offenders if they are professional) is automatically close enough to the crime scene to become a suspect based on a psychological based criminal profile or psychologically based conjecture.

3.   Of course, law enforcement would be double negligent if a predictable homicide occurred and the FBI's behavioral science unit prevented the homicide from being solved.

4.   For example, the *Homicides in Chicago, 1965-1994* data indicate that about 20% of homicides in Chicago between the years 1981 and 1994 are committed by youth gangs. Perhaps this percentage can be considered a rough approximation for the nation as a whole. See, C. R. Block, R. L. Block, and the Illinois Criminal Justice Information Authority. *Homicides in Chicago*, 1965-

1994, [Computer file]. 2nd ICPSR version. (Ann Arbor, MI: Inter-university Consortium for Political and Social Research [distributor], ICPSR 6399, 1996).

5.   The increased broad based education of police is not a new recommendation. See for example, J. J. Senna and L. J. Siegil, *Introduction to Criminal Justice* 2d ed. (St. Paul: West Publishing Co., 1981), 139-40 and 240-242.

6.   The empirical and theoretical analysis provided in earlier chapters suggests the rule of inapplicability. To be sure, those with vested interests in profiling can usually construe facts to create an "exception" to the rule. Unfortunately, that is also be misleading.

7.   This output would correspond closely to homicide clearance rates. Each year the homicide clearance rate – the ratio of homicides cleared by arrest or other exceptional means to homicides detected and reported – is reported in the Uniform Crime Reports of the FBI.

8.   See J. Douglas and M. Olshaker, *Mindhunter: Inside the FBI's Elite Serial Crime Unit* (New York: Simon & Schuster, 1996).

9.   On the other hand, increased police training in the area of professional homicide offenders may more than offset the need for additional specialized resources.

10.   Court production systems appear to be very non-standardized. This implies that technical efficiency in court production is very unlikely. In the short-run, the level of resources available for prosecution is, therefore, a very important consideration.

BIBLIOGRAPHY

Andreoni, J. "Criminal Deterrence in the Reduced Form: A New Perspective on Ehrlich's Seminal Study," *Economic Inquiry* 33 (July 1995): 476-483.

Battalio R. C. et al., "A Test of Consumer Demand Theory Using Observations of Individual Purchases," *Western Economic Journal* (December 1973): 411-428.

Becker, G. S. "Crime and Punishment: An Economic Approach," *Journal of Political Economy* 76 (March-April 1968): 169-217.

―――. *Accounting for Tastes*. Cambridge: Harvard University Press, 1996.

Block, C. R., R. L. Block, and the Illinois Criminal Justice Information Authority. *Homicides in Chicago, 1965-1994* [Computer file]. 2nd ICPSR version. Chicago, IL: Illinois Criminal Justice Information Authority [producer], 1996. Ann Arbor, MI: Inter-university Consortium for Political and Social Research [distributor], 1996.

Block, M. K., and J. Heineke, "A Labor Theoretical Analysis of the Criminal Choice," *American Economic Review* 65 (June 1975): 314-325.

Corvasce, M. V., and J. R. Paglino, *Murder One: A Writer's Guide to Homicide*. Cincinnati: Writer's Digest Books, 1997.

Darrough, M. N., and J. M. Heineke. *The Multi-Output Translog Production Cost Function: The Case of Law Enforcement Agencies*. In *Economic Models of Criminal Behavior*, ed. J. M. Heineke, 259-302. Amsterdam: North Holland, 1978.

DiIulio, J. J. "The Black Crime Gap," *The Wall Street Journal*, 11 July 1994, sec. A, p. 10.

Douglas, J., R. Ressler, A. Burgess, and C. Hartman, "Criminal Profiling from Crime Scene Analysis," *Behavioral Sciences and the Law* 4, no. 4 (1986): 401-421.

Douglas, J., and M. Olshaker. *Mindhunter: Inside the FBI's Elite Serial Crime Unit*. New York: Simon & Schuster, 1996.

Ehrlich, I. "The Deterrent Effect of Capital Punishment: A Question of Life and Death," *American Economic Review* 65 (June 1975): 397-417.

Felson, R. B. "Impression Management and the Escalation of Aggression and Violence," *Social Psychology Quarterly* 45, no. 4 (1982): 245-254.

Felson, R. B., S. A. Ribner, and M. S. Siegel, "Age and the Effect of Third Parties During Criminal Violence," *Sociology and Social Research* 68, no. 4 (1984): 452-462.

Felson, R. B., and H. J. Steadman, "Situational Factors in Disputes Leading to Criminal Violence," *Criminology* 21 (February 1983): 59-74.

Fleisher, M. *Beggars and Thieves*. Milwaukee: University of Wisconsin Press, 1995.

Fox, J. A., and G. L. Pierce, *Uniform Crime Reports [United States]: Supplementary Homicide Reports, 1976-1983*. Ann Arbor, MI: Inter-university Consortium for Political and Social Research, ICPSR 8657, 1987.

Furlong, W. J. "The Deterrent Effect of Regulatory Enforcement in the Fishery," *Land Economics* 67 (February 1991): 116-129.

Grogger, J. "Certainty v. Severity of Punishment," *Economic Inquiry* 29 (April 1991): 297-309.

Gylys, J. "Application of a Production Function to Police Patrol Activity," *The Police Chief* (July 1974): 70-72.

Hellman, D. A., and J. L. Naroff, *The Urban Public Sector and Urban Crime: A Simultaneous System Approach.* Washington: U. S. Government Printing Office, 1980.

Hey, J. D. *Uncertainty in Microeconomics.* New York: New York University Press, 1979.

Hull, B. B., and F. Bold, "Preaching Matters: Replication and Extension," *Journal of Economic Behavior and Organization* 27 (June 1995): 143-149.

Kleck, G. "Racial Discrimination in Criminal Sentencing: A Critical Evaluation of the Evidence with Additional Evidence on the Death Penalty," *American Sociological Review* 46 (December 1981): 783-805.

Kuhn, T. "Blast meant to intimidate, Babbit says," *The Arizona Republic*, 3 June 1976, sec. A., p. 19.

Marché, G. E. *The Economics of Law Enforcement: Production Comparisons Between Large and Small Police Unites.* Ann Arbor, Mich.: University Microforms, 1990.

———, "Aggregation Biases and Economies of Scale in the Metropolitan Police Unit Production Function," *Review of Social Economy* 1 (Summer 1992): 215-233.

———. "The Production of Homicide Solutions: An Empirical Analysis," *American Journal of Economics and Sociology* 53 (October 1994): 385-401.

———. "Mending a Hole in the Police Dragnet: A Criminal Profile for Rationally Motivated Homicides," *Forensics: TEJ* The Electronic On-line Journal of the American College of Forensic Examiners (Spring 1996).

McCann, J. T. "Criminal Personality Profiling in the Investigation of Violent Crime: Recent Advances and Future Directions," *Behavioral Sciences and the Law* 10, no. 4 (1992): 475-481.

Messner, S. F. "Regional Differences in the Economic Correlates of the Urban Homicide Rate: Some Evidence on the Importance of Cultural Context," *Criminology* 21 (November 1983): 177-188.

Murphy, W., and J. Peters, "Profiling Child Sexual Abuses: Psychological Considerations," *Criminal Justice and Behavior* 19 (March 1992): 24-37.

Pinker, S. *How the Mind Works.* New York: W. W. Norton & Company, 1997.

Pinnizzotto, A. J., and N. J. Finkel, "Criminal Personality Profiling: An Outcome and Process Study," *Law and Human Behavior* 14 (June 1990): 215-233.

Ressler, R. K. et al., "Sexual Killers and Their Victims: Identifying Patterns Through Crime Scene Analysis," *Journal of Interpersonal Violence* 1 (September 1986): 288-253.

Ryans, M. R. "The Irresistible Impulse in the Lorena Bobbitt Case," *Forensic Examiner* 5 (September - October 1996): 11-12.

Scalice, V. "White House Counsel, Vincent Foster Case Reopened," *Forensic Examiner* 4 (September - October 1995): 13-15.

Senna, J. J., and L. J. Siegil. *Introduction to Criminal Justice* 2d ed. St. Paul: West Publishing Co., 1981.

Silberberg, E. *The Structure of Economics: A Mathematical Analysis.* New York: McGraw-Hill Book Company, 1978.

Sollars, D. L., B. L. Benson, and D. W. Rasmussen, "Drug Enforcement and the Deterrence of Property Crime Among Local Jurisdictions," *Public Finance Quarterly* 22 (January 1994): 22-45.

Turco, R. N. "Psychological Profiling," *International Journal of Offender Therapy and Comparative Criminology* 34, no. 2 (1990): 147-154.

Wilson, J. Q. *Thinking About Crime* rev. ed. New York: Basic Books, 1983.

222